The World According to

GOGGLEBOX

Published in Great Britain in 2014 by Canongate Books Ltd, 14 High Street,
Edinburgh EH1 1TE

www.canongate.tv

1

Text and photography © Studio Lambert
Programme and format © Studio Lambert
Foreword © Craig Cash and Caroline Aherne, 2014

The moral right of the author has been asserted

Design © Unreal Ltd, 2014
Illustrations © Quinton Winter

Additional photography
Page 208 © Shutterstock
Page 231 © Jason Hazeley
Page 232 © BBC Photo Library
Page 234 © Tony Larkin/Rex

British Library Cataloguing-in-Publication Data
A catalogue record for this book is available on
request from the British Library.

ISBN 978 1 78211 489 5
Export ISBN 978 1 78211 598 4

Printed and bound in Italy by Lego S.p.A.

The World According to

GOGGLEBOX

Jason Hazeley and Joel Morris

Foreword by
Craig Cash and Caroline Aherne

Illustrations by
Quinton Winter

CANONGATE
Edinburgh · London

5

FOREWORD
Caroline Aherne and Craig Cash

Imagine watching Jim Royle watching *Gogglebox*.

'Barbara, have you seen this shite? They're expecting us to watch people we've never even heard of, sat around watching TV and carping on about it. Who in their right mind would do that, Barb? *Gogglebox*, my arse!'

The following Friday at 9 p.m. you're watching *Gogglebox*, where the wonderful regulars are watching *The Royle Family* watching them and saying something much funnier than we could ever write. It could happen. It probably will one day, once we get over the fact that the child we have spawned is much funnier than we are. We could never have written Leon and June sat watching as the titles to *When Corden Met Barlow* rolled.

LEON: Who's Barlow?

JUNE: Gary Barlow!

LEON: Oh no. TWO dickheads!

Gogglebox is not only properly funny, it's also brave, true, heartwarming and heartbreaking. Each episode is assembled with a remarkable deftness of touch and a clear fondness for each of the participants.

When so much TV would have us believe that Britain is broken, you only have to watch *Gogglebox* to realise that it isn't broken at all. It's alive and well, with the biggest and warmest of hearts.

A work of sheer genius.

Caroline Aherne and Craig Cash
(Sat on a sofa, pissed up with Steph and Dom)

x

PREFACE

Tania Alexander

Jim Royle's likely dismissive scoffing at an episode of *Gogglebox* is pretty much the reaction a lot of people had when we presented them with the idea of a TV show where we watch people watching television. To them, it seemed like the moment when TV was about to eat itself whole and regurgitate the contents of its own stomach across the screen.

But that was, of course, before they'd seen a single frame of it.

Gogglebox required us to believe in one simple notion: that the great British public knows best when it comes to what the television makers serve up. The moment when it became clear that this very simple idea would work was when we filmed our very first audition with one particular Liverpudlian family. The family consisted of Mum, Dad and two grown-up twentysomething children still living at home. Talking to them in their living room, while they watched telly, a producer asked them what they thought the BBC stood for – as in its values. The following conversation unfolded, unprompted…

DAUGHTER (25): Er, B…B…C… Well, it stands for British Broadcasting…er …Company. Doesn't it?

SON (29): No…British…Broad…casting…Corporation.

DAUGHTER: NO! That's not right, 'cause then it would be BBCC!

The son rolled his eyes.

DAUGHTER: So what does ITV stand for then? Inter…national Television?

DAD (employing a slightly weary tone): No, you div, Independent Television.

The daughter looked down, and paused momentarily. Then, as if a light bulb had just been switched on in her head, she looked up and with a huge smile gleefully announced…

'Oh, that's brilliant, that is…so those mings at Channel 4…they couldn't even be arsed coming up with a mammogram!'

Cue further rolling of eyes and groaning from parents and brother alike.

It was this moment when we knew that *Gogglebox* would work. Not just because of the unintentional humour involved, but because of the remarkable interaction that occurs when we sit down with the people we love to watch television.

Sadly, the family mentioned elected not to take part in the series, and I often wonder what they make of it. Then again, the current cast of *Gogglebox* have delighted us week in, week out with far more priceless gems of genuine wit, wisdom and heartfelt humanity, so much more than I could ever have imagined.

For me, *Gogglebox* belongs to each and every one of them, and so does this book.

Tania Alexander
Executive Producer of Channel 4's *Gogglebox*

JOSH: Do you think Japanese people will become extinct?

 BILL: Snakes have two penises, don't they?

 LEON: They're all strange, people who do allotments.

 STEPHEN: If they're going to make mannequins more realistic, give them bingo wings.

 SANDRA: What's inside a penis? Meat?

 JUNE: You shouldn't split things with a swear word, Leon.

 DOM: I very nearly got my nipple pierced in Ireland on my stag weekend. Thank God it was shut.

 STEPHEN: Well, that's bored the shit out of me arse.

 SCARLETT: He is beautiful, isn't he? His face looks like it's been carved by angels.

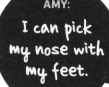

BAASIT: Do you know that a beaver can kill a man? It chomps down on you and can cut the femoral artery.

 JUNE: Do you remember the time when we were invited out and you threw up on somebody's carpet?

 LEON: Yes. He's dead now, isn't he?

 LINDA: How do they know what's going to be the weather? Do they measure something?

 DOM: 'What did you do in the office today, darling?'
'I wanked a walrus.'

 UMAR: What's a micropenis?

 STEPHEN: Where do they find these people from? She looks like fucking Ken Dodd.

 LINDA: I know a man named Hitler. You'd think he'd change his name, wouldn't you?

 BAASIT: I've like rushed home to go to the toilet, but never to watch a programme about toilets.

 STEPH: I thought the world was going to explode when we ran out of gin.

 BILL: You know Alfred Hitchcock didn't have a belly button, don't you?

 LEON: I want a Smartphone.

 JUNE: Leon, you're not smart enough to have a Smartphone.

SANDRA: The last time I saw a tub of Vaseline I wasn't very happy when I saw it.

 STEPHEN: I love Dave. We named our dildo after him.

 BAASIT: The further north you go, the more bear-like women look. I'm sure there's been studies done in that.

 LEON: Didn't I go out with a girl who was in for Miss Shell Oil Refinery?

 UMAR: One of Hull's problems is that it's called Hull.

 VIV: I wanted to be on *Jim'll Fix It*. I'm very glad Jim didn't fix it for me, I'm telling you. Ugh.

 STEPHEN: She's gone out looking for a meteorite, but she's fucking minge-deep in snow.

 LINDA: What's the best birthday you've ever had?

 PETE: You had laryngitis once.

 SANDRA: I love *Antique Roadshow*. Posh car boot sale.

 LOUIS: Baldrick, time has not been good to you, my friend.

 UMAR: What do you call a Pakistani guy standing in between two houses?

 SID: I don't know.

 UMAR: Ali.

DOM: I'll end up negative equity, you'll take the house back, I'll probably end up in prison playing hide the sausage with Mad Axeman Mallard.

 STEPHEN: I ain't going to fucking Harvester for Christmas dinner.

 LOUIS: The bigger the mug, the more important the family member.

 STEPH: Thank God that's over. Phew. Can we watch some porn now?

 **LEON:** Well, if we had to evacuate the house, there's not really much I'd take, I couldn't get my television out. So the only thing I'd save would be you, darling. I'd put you on my back and carry you out.

LEON:

If I was trick-or-treating, my trick would be mooning.

June & Leon
Liverpool

Leon & June

LIVERPOOL

———

Leon, 79, and June, 77, have been married for 54 years. They are both retired teachers. Leon taught History (to Wayne Rooney's aunts and uncles, among others) and June taught English (to Willy Russell's children, among others). Leon is a keen bridge player, and June enjoys swimming. They have two daughters and three grandchildren.

———

HOW DID YOU MEET?

LEON: Teacher training college, 1955. I'd just done National Service in the army and you came from South Wales. And there was this beautiful girl… and that was it.

JUNE: We had to be in at 10.30 at night. And nobody broke the rules, or you were sent down for three days. We liked the big bands in those days, and they used to come to the town halls, and we used to go. But you had to ask permission. You had to be on the last bus back: it dropped you in the village at quarter to twelve, and you were in before midnight. And you had to have a signed pass.

LEON: It was very hard with my parents, though, because I'm Jewish and June isn't. So we had murders before we could get married.

JUNE: Leon's an only child, so it was very difficult for his parents to come to terms with.

LEON: But in the end we won through, didn't we?

JUNE: Once they realised that we were determined to get married with or without their blessing, they came to terms with it.

LEON: We used to watch *Coronation Street* with my parents.

JUNE: That's right. Your mother started watching it and said, 'Oh, you've got to come over and watch it.' We'd been married about six months.

LEON: And we finally got a television.

JUNE: Rented, in those days. Leon did nights at play centres after school to pay the television rental. And then, when we had the children there were always good programmes on Sunday teatime – *Anne of Green Gables, Little Women…*

LEON: *Wind in the Willows.*

JUNE: And we'd sit with the children and have a picnic tea. We had a travel rug, and we used to pretend we were outside. They used to do their homework and we used to do our marking all at the same time in various parts of the house. And then it was, right, it's tea, everybody's finished, everything's away, we're all going to do this together. I've always made a point where we eat together and we watch some TV together.

JUNE:

We started watching Dr Who with the kids.

17

HOW DID YOU GET ON GOGGLEBOX?

LEON: I'm a member of Liverpool Bridge Club and last year two girls came in looking for people. And I got talking to them, and they said, 'This programme's coming out – are you interested?'

JUNE: He always comes home with a story. He said, 'Guess what? Somebody from TV was there today.' I said, right. (I thought he meant playing bridge.) He said, 'We could be on TV.' I said, don't be ridiculous. And he goes on and on and on about it. I thought, it's such a simple idea, it's not going to catch on.

BEING RECOGNISED

LEON: We were getting hugged in John Lewis yesterday.

JUNE: We went down to London to see the tennis last November. And this woman came up and said, 'Hi, June. How are you?' I said, 'Hello.' And she said, 'Where's Leon?'

I just couldn't believe it. After that, we were stopped probably a dozen times that day. I mean, I'm not surprised in Liverpool, because Liverpool love their own, but London? We were just staggered.

LEON: We saw Anna Ivanovich play Venus Williams. Ivanovich was wearing red knickers.

 JANE: I love you Leon, but please keep your clothes on. @LeonAndJune #**Gogglebox**

WHAT DO YOU THINK
OF YOURSELVES ON SCREEN?

LEON: I think, 'My wife's still beautiful.' For your sixtieth I took you to Vienna and Salzburg. Wonderful, absolutely wonderful, Salzburg. We waltzed onto the balcony in Vienna, didn't we?

JUNE: Yes.

LEON: To Strauss...

JUNE: I wasn't happy about the 'Show Us Your Knicks' thing.

LEON: You've always looked gorgeous in your knicks. And your bottom's nice as well. I mentioned that.

JUNE: What you see on TV is what we really are.

LEON: I say what I like.

JUNE: And we're used to performing, I suppose. And as a teacher, you perform in every lesson. You've got to sell your subject. If you don't, those young people are going to have a bleak future.

LEON: I always thought I was brilliant anyway.

JUNE: If you tell Leon to say something, he'll immediately say the opposite, just to be perverse. And Leon has the most grotesque clothes. You know, sometimes I stand in the hall and say, we're not going out with you dressed like that. You can wear it to bridge. With all your lovely ladies.

LEON:

I always thought I was brilliant anyway.

Leon and June with 'our Helen' (left) and 'our Julie' (right), taken on Julie's first birthday, January 1966.

WHAT DO YOU LIKE WATCHING?

LEON: I like watching stuff that makes me laugh. I'll go in the other room and watch Gold. Victor Meldrew (who I'm compared to), Hyacinth Bucket, *The Likely Lads, Last of the Summer Wine*… I love all those. *Have I Got News For You*. We love that.

JUNE: And *Would I Lie To You?*

LEON: Rob Brydon.

JUNE: I like Rageh Omaar. I like Hazel Irvine, who does the snooker. And Julie Walters. She's great at whatever she does.

LEON: Brilliant. And Miranda Hart. Love her. I don't fancy her, but she's very funny. Her expressions. And the way she throws herself on the floor. And *Jeeves and Wooster*.

JUNE: Hugh Laurie's very talented, isn't he?

LEON: *Frasier*. I love him. I watch him every morning and I've seen them all.

JUNE: He's got the box set.

LEON: Martin, the father, he's got a chair like me.

JUNE: I can't decide who he is: Victor Meldrew or Martin.

LEON: I used to like Bill Turnbull on Breakfast. Then I found out he was at public school. So he's off the list.

LEON:

I like Gabby Yorath. And Gaby Roslin. The Gabbies.

22

WHAT TV DO YOU DISAGREE ON?

LEON: *Sharpe* is my favourite.

JUNE: Now, I won't watch that.

LEON: Sean Bean is brilliant.

JUNE: I don't like anything with war. Particularly if it's battle scenes and things – I don't like anything like that. That's why I never liked history at school: because we always did wars and it's quite graphic on TV. I feel physically sick when I watch it.

LEON: *Diners, Drive-Ins And Dives.*

JUNE: That's awful.

LEON: Because I'm a big eater, and they're throwing onions in, and steaks and chickens – incredible.

JUNE: Heart attack on a plate.

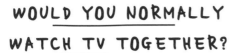

WOULD YOU NORMALLY WATCH TV TOGETHER?

LEON: I'm in charge of the remote. She takes it off me occasionally.

JUNE: As a fellow at work once said, 'Leave us with the remote, it's the only power we males have these days.'

WHAT DOES TV MEAN TO YOU?

LEON: Television can involve you. You become part of it. It's entertainment. And it's company for old people, who love a lot of the programmes. I hate people who say, 'Oh, I never watch television.' I mean, what's wrong with you, pal? I hate people who say they don't drink. That annoys me as well.

JUNE: At our age we have a lot of friends who are on their own – they've lost their wives or husbands. And they say, particularly in the winter when it's dark, they draw the curtains and the only person they have a relationship with is the television in the corner.

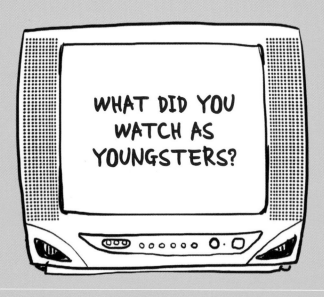

STEPH & DOM, SANDWICH

 STEPH: Basil Brush made me laugh. And Frank Spencer.

 DOM: *The Goodies. The Banana Splits.* 'One banana, two banana, three banana, four…'

 STEPH: 'La la la…' I'm there now.

 DOM: And *On the Buses.*

 STEPH: *On the Buses?* Are you mad?

 DOM: No. Not *On the Buses.* The kids' programme, *The Double Deckers.*

 STEPH: I liked *The Herbs.*

 DOM: *The Magic Roundabout.* Dylan was always…

 STEPH: Off his tits. But Sooty and all that lot? No. Oh, and *Rainbow?* Forget it. Zippy. Christ. Zip it up and throw it away.

 DOM: *Batman.* Pow and kazam! And Hartley Hare from *Pipkins* was OK when I was ill.

 STEPH: When you put your thermometer on the radiator. Do you remember that? 'A temperature of 120?' 'I'm really ill! I really am!' 'Yep, you're dead.'

> **CHRIS:**
> When I was growing up, until about the age of nine we had a black-and-white TV. Everyone else on the estate had colour TVs.

STEPHEN & CHRIS, BRIGHTON

 CHRIS: *Blind Date. Surprise Surprise.*

 STEPHEN: We were allowed to stay up late to watch *Dallas.* But back then, we didn't have a pot to piss in and we had a TV that had a pay box on it. And you used to put 50p in it and wind it on, and that would give you four hours' worth of viewing. And you'd get a collection of 50ps in the box. The man would come and empty it once a month, take out the rental (because we rented the TV), take a bit out for the licence fee, and what was left you got back.

Dallas went out on a Wednesday night at eight. So, we were allowed to stay up for that. But sometimes we didn't have another 50p, so we'd miss the end of *Dallas*. And if Mum had no more money, to entertain us she used to take her teeth out and gurn. And we would all roll about laughing and then go to bed.

When I was very young, I watched *Magic Roundabout, Rainbow*, the man that used to go in the cupboard in the fancy dress shop… *Mr Benn*. Loved that.

 CHRIS: Because I'm five years younger than you it was all Phillip Schofield, you know, in the broom cupboard.

 STEPHEN: See, I was out joyriding by then.

THE MICHAELS, BRIGHTON

 ANDREW: *Watch with Mother* – that I did actually used to watch with my mother.

 CAROLYNE: So did I.

 ANDREW: My favourite one was *The Flowerpot Men*. And my second favourite was *Andy Pandy*. And as a five-year-old, I actually used to look forward to the bit where he gets in the basket at the end with Looby Loo, because I knew there was something going on.

 CAROLYNE: In the basket.

 ANDREW: I didn't know what it was at five, but I was bloody sure there was something going on.

 CAROLYNE: When we first met, that was our frame of reference, wasn't it? You were Andy Pandy and I was Looby Loo.

ANDREW: Do you remember the Jaguar XJS? I used to get the Looby Loo that was you and hang it up in the XJS. But in addition to the two that I've just mentioned, *Stingray, Joe 90, Captain Scarlet, Thunderbirds, Lost in Space* and *Star Trek*.

 CAROLYNE: I used to look forward to watching *Top of the Pops*, because that was the only time we'd ever get to see any groups, wasn't it?

 ANDREW: Don't think I ever watched one episode of *Top of the Pops*.

 CAROLYNE: Oh! *Blue Peter*! I got a *Blue Peter* badge. For complaining.

 ANDREW: Did you?

 CAROLYNE: They gave it to me as a consolation prize because I came down to Brighton to see Valerie Singleton, Peter Purves and John Noakes. I was a massive fan of *Blue Peter*. Every week, when they used to get the Fairy Liquid bottles out, I used to make everything. I was there with all my cereal boxes and polystyrene and that sticky back plastic.

Well, I came down to see them on the London to Brighton – I must have been about nine or ten – and I was so excited to meet them, to go and say hello and get their autographs. And I went up to the car where they were and I think they had minders or something. And they just pushed me away and said, 'Oh no, no, go away, you can't meet the presenters,' and I was so, so upset. I wrote a letter to the BBC and so, as a consolation prize, I got a letter signed by all the *Blue Peter* cast, and a *Blue Peter* badge. I really liked Peter Purves, I have to say. John Noakes I wasn't so keen on, perhaps because he wasn't so good-looking.

LOUIS: I remember a time when we were watching a film and there was a sex scene or something like that. And I was nine or ten, quite young, and Mum was trying to put her hands over my eyes. And I was thinking, get back, woman. I have to grow up some time.

 ANDREW: When's that time going to come?

 CAROLYNE: Yeah. We're still waiting.

 LOUIS: I sometimes put my hands over my own eyes. Still can't deal with it.

SANDY & SANDRA, BRIXTON

 SANDY: *Joe 90. Magic Roundabout. Button Moon.*

 SANDRA: *The Osmonds. Hawaii Five-O. Kojak.*

 SANDY: *CHiPs. Stingray!*

 SANDRA: 'Mariiiii-naaaa... Aquamariiiii-naaaaa...'

 SANDY: *Bionic Woman.*

 SANDRA: All them hardcore things made us as we are today. We didn't do *Bill and Ben* and *Humpty Dumpty*.

THE MOFFATTS, COUNTY DURHAM

 MARK: My favourite cartoon when I was a kid was *Marine Boy*.

 BETTY: I used to like things like *The Famous Five*, and *Worzel Gummidge* and *Doctor Who*, even though I was scared of it then.

SCARLETT: *Noddy. Johnny Bravo. CatDog. Goosebumps. Robot Wars.*

 MARK: We used to love *Robot Wars.*

 SCARLETT: Oh, me and my dad were seriously going to do it, weren't we? We were going to get stuff from work so that we could make one. But we ended up just buying the crappy ones that you made.

 BETTY: They used to love *Robot Wars.*

 MARK: With Craig Charles off *Red Dwarf.* Used to love *Red Dwarf.*

 SCARLETT: Ah, *Red Dwarf.* Well, actually, as a kid, I am a bit weird, like, I really liked *The Young Ones, Red Dwarf, Bottom, The Thin Blue Line,* stuff like that. Stuff that my friends didn't really get, and were, like, 'What is this?' Because, when I was little, I used to go to my nan's and I used to watch things like Norman Wisdom and stuff. So I'm a bit weird like that.

THE TAPPERS, NORTH LONDON

 JONATHAN: I used to like *Tiswas.* With Spit the Dog. And *Digby, the Biggest Dog in the World.* And *The Littlest Hobo.* I loved dogs.

 NIKKI: 'Down the road, that's where I want to beeee…' And I loved *Jim'll Fix It.* Shhh. And Jonathan loved *Star Wars* when he was a kid. I just do not get *Star Wars.* It's the most boring thing.

 JONATHAN: No. *Star Wars* is brilliant.

 NIKKI: When the kids saw it, Josh just wanted to know where it was set.

 JOSH: I didn't know it was meant to be set on another planet like *Avatar* is or…I don't know, like a fantasy planet. Or two separate planets and they fought in space.

 JONATHAN: *Star Wars.* It's set in the stars.

REV. KATE & GRAHAM, NOTTINGHAMSHIRE

 GRAHAM: Well, obviously, my parents were so middle-class we didn't even have a telly.

 KATE: Grew up without a telly.

 GRAHAM: No cultural references.

 KATE: So, a lot of the time I'll say things like, oh, *Chorlton and the Wheelies* – and Graham will go, 'What?' So, when I'm introducing my kids to stuff, I sometimes have to introduce Graham too. I'll go, 'Do you not remember this?' And he'll go, 'I didn't watch telly in the 70s.' But what about the TV that you sneaked into the vicarage?

 GRAHAM: Oh yeah. I mended a telly and just put it in my room.

 KATE: And your mum used to come in and watch tennis on it when your dad wasn't looking.

 GRAHAM: One day, Dad said, 'You shouldn't have that – you haven't got a licence.' I went, 'I've just bought one.'

 KATE: He bought his own TV licence.

 GRAHAM: Mum said, 'I think you should get rid of it.' I said, but you've just been watching tennis for the past two hours, so are you sure about that? The next week they went out and bought a colour telly.

LINDA, PETE & GEORGE, CLACTON-ON-SEA

 LINDA: *Lassie.* I used to just cry my eyes out at *Lassie.*

 PETE: *Grandstand.*

 LINDA: See, we're so different.

THE X FACTOR

THE MICHAELS, BRIGHTON

ANDREW: It's like a Victorian freak show.

THE SIDDIQUIS, DERBY

BAASIT: Jesus Christ, man. One million people haven't got anything better to do on a Sunday night.

THE TAPPERS, NORTH LONDON

AMY: What does the 'X' stand for? Xylophone?

THE SIDDIQUIS, DERBY

BAASIT: You know it's a shit performance when the first thing Dermot pays compliment to is the stage.

STEPHEN & CHRIS, BRIGHTON

STEPHEN: Nicole's put too much bloody baby oil on, hasn't she? She looks like someone's just come over her. Look, she's all jizzy.

THE VOICE

THE MOFFATTS, COUNTY DURHAM

SCARLETT: I bet George Michael's turning in his bloody grave.

STEPHEN & CHRIS, BRIGHTON

STEPHEN: It's enough to give your arsehole a headache.

THE WOERDENWEBERS, THE WIRRAL

RALF: It's like karaoke after twenty pints.

BRITAIN'S GOT TALENT

THE MOFFATTS, COUNTY DURHAM

SCARLETT: The first thing that I do whenever they come on *Britain's Got Talent* is Google the name. And 90 per cent of the time they've worked on cruise ships, they've done big gigs, they've won talent contests before. And I'm just like, this is not fair. And you should never know the sob stories.

MARK: Everybody's got a sob story.

SCARLETT: I feel like TV lies to us. I do. That's why I like doing *Gogglebox* – because people have an opinion of everybody. And then, when they get to watch you a little bit more, they get to see the real you.

STEPH & DOM, SANDWICH

STEPH: Can you imagine the interviews? 'Have you had any shit in your life? Have you lost any parents? Give us your worst shit and then you might be worth putting out.'

CLARE BALDING
The good thing about not having seen *Britain's Got Talent* when it went out is that it's even more fun via
#Gogglebox

COUNTDOWN

 BAASIT: I hate Dictionary Corner. They're a right bunch of know-it-alls. They've got a flipping dictionary in front of them; of course they're going to get it.

 JUNE: Passion: P-A-S-S-I-O-N.

 LEON: Piss is on as well: P-I-S-S.

DEAL OR NO DEAL

THE SIDDIQUIS, DERBY

 UMAR: Noel Edmonds is a game show host of things that aren't game shows. They all say they've got a strategy. What's the strategy? Just pick a box. It's ridiculous. And there's no banker there on the other line.

THE WOERDENWEBERS, THE WIRRAL

 VIV: I'd go on *Deal or No Deal*. Yeah, I have a strategy actually. I know what boxes I'd pick. 'Cause I play it on the phone.

SANDY & SANDRA, BRIXTON

 SANDY: I can't do it. I only learnt it the other day. I think it's boring. I can't be arsed waiting for the banker to tell me this and tell me that. And don't get it twisted. The banker's always going to be right. They always say it's like gambling, isn't it? Casinos always end up winning in the end.

STEPHEN: No deal.

JUNE: Switch it off.

VIV:

Stephen & Chris
Brighton

Stephen & Chris

BRIGHTON

—

Stephen, 43, and Chris, 38, are hairdressers
and first met eleven years ago. Stephen spends
a lot of time at Chris's bungalow near Brighton,
where they love a takeaway in front of the telly.
Chris shares his home (and often his sofa)
with his enormous cat, Ginge.

HOW DID YOU MEET?

STEPHEN: We were working in the same salon as each other about eleven or twelve years ago. Then he left and went somewhere else, and I left, and when I came back to Brighton about three years ago, we met up with each other again.

CHRIS: You started chatting to me on Grindr, didn't you?

STEPHEN: Yeah. And we started seeing each other. But it didn't really work out. It finished just after the first series. It was only four episodes, but it fucking ruined it.

I do take the piss out of him a lot and I think, when we were together, you took it to heart a bit, didn't you?

CHRIS: Yeah. Because the thing is, if you're supposed to love someone, why would you rip the piss out of them the whole time?

STEPHEN: Entertainment, dear.

CHRIS: For you. Not for me.

STEPHEN: There's twenty-four hours in a day: I get bored. But it did make me feel bad because I felt like a bully.

CHRIS: We're much better as friends, anyway.

STEPHEN: I still take the piss as much, but you just say, 'Shut up.'

CHRIS:

If you're supposed to love someone, why would you rip the piss out of them the whole time?

HOW DID YOU GET ON GOGGLEBOX?

CHRIS: This woman walked into the salon and said she was looking for someone to take part in a TV programme, so I went running over and went, 'Oh my God! Tell me about it! Tell me about it!'

STEPHEN: Fame-hungry bitch. I wasn't interested at first. I just thought, it will sink without trace. And then he said, 'They're paying us,' and I went, 'All right, I'll do it.'

Chris and Ginge, the big pussy

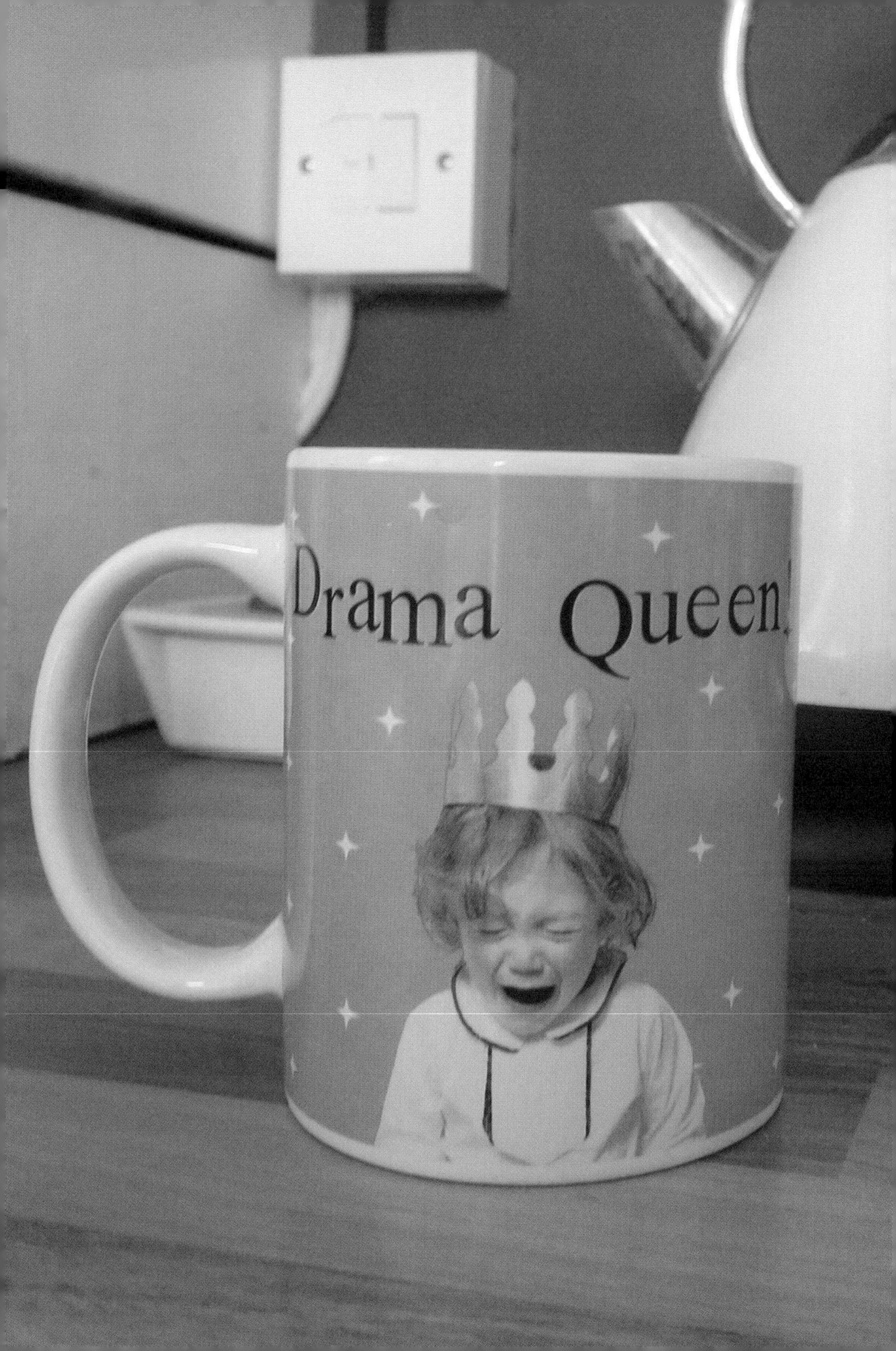
Drama Queen

WHAT DO YOU THINK OF YOURSELVES ON SCREEN?

CHRIS: It was a bit strange at first, because I think people had said, 'You've got to be careful what you say, because you're going to be on TV, it's going to be out there,' so in the first one I was really quiet. And people were, like, 'That's not you.' But you overanalyse things in your head and you think, I can't say that because you know, it might go on TV and I don't want people to think that I'm nasty or I'm rude or…

STEPHEN: I didn't give a fuck.

CHRIS: Yeah, but you don't give a fuck anyway.

WHAT WAS YOUR FAMILY'S REACTION?

CHRIS: My sisters absolutely love it. Tune in every single week.

STEPHEN: All my family watch it, and I'll say something and they'll go, 'Oh, that's something your nan used to say,' or, 'Oh my God, you looked like your brother when you said that.' So they've said it's like watching them, because we're all pretty much the same character, our family.

CHRIS: Oh God, yeah. A bit inbred. You all look the same.

BEING RECOGNISED

STEPHEN: When we did the first series, I didn't have a Twitter account, nor did Chris. And someone said to us, 'Why don't you get a Twitter account?' So we opened it up, and I think within two days it was, like, 7,000 followers – and it's just gone up and up and up. I think we're up to about 60,000 now.

CHRIS: Well, you are. I'm up to about 47,000.

STEPHEN: And out of all the Tweets I've had, I've only ever got two crap ones. One was a bit weird and said she wanted to fuck me mum. My mum was, like, 'Does she? Get her round here. I'll fuck her up.' That one, she got chucked out of Iceland's. There's a picture of her, on her Twitter page, being carried out of Iceland's.

In real life, people are brilliant. I don't suppose I've ever been so popular. You know, you walk into a bar and everyone's really nice. Everyone. Not one person has said... Oh, actually, the other day I was in Hurstpierpoint and this car went past, it slowed down and the window went down. And the bloke went, 'Oi, mate! Are you the geezer off the telly?' And I went, 'Yeah.' And he went, 'You're a wanker!' I really started laughing, and I went, 'I know!' And he laughed and drove off.

CHRIS: I've had all really good responses as well. But I was out a couple of weeks ago, and this woman came running over to me, waving at me, and she was, like, 'Oh my God!

I love you on the TV. Can I have my picture taken with you?' And I was, like, 'Yeah, course.' I sat down with her and one of her friends was trying to take the picture. Then, all of a sudden, this guy came over and tapped me on the shoulder and went, 'Someone's sitting there.' And I said, 'I'm just having a picture done with her.' And he was, like, 'Yeah, but you don't get what I'm saying: someone's sitting there.' And I went 'Yeah, I know. I'm going to be moving in a minute. She wanted to talk to me.'

And then I got another tap on my other shoulder – and it was her husband. And he went, 'That's my fucking missus.' And I went, 'She's called me over here because she likes me on *Gogglebox*. I'm only having a picture taken with her, then I'm going...'

STEPHEN: 'And I'm as bent as a nine-bob note...'

CHRIS: Why would I be interested in her? We were in a gay bar. But the thing was, the rest of the night all they did was just throw me the evils.

STEPHEN: But I love it. On a Saturday night, when you're out and you've had a load of drink, it's brilliant. Sunday morning, when you've got a hangover – stranger danger and beer fear – that's when I start getting paranoid, thinking that someone's going to be horrible or something.

> **STEPHEN:**
> Well, the camera don't f***ing love me.

BEING RECOGNISED (continued)

There's a woman who works on the road
I work on, and she said to me,
'You really do look better in the flesh.'
I thought, you cheeky cow.

CHRIS: You see, I get the opposite.
Some of my really close friends are,
like, 'Oh my God, Chris, you look so
good on TV.' And I'm, like – I don't in
real life? 'Well, yeah, you look nice
in real life, but on TV you look really hot.'

STEPHEN:
F*** knows how
I get away with
it. I used to lay
tarmac before
I hairdressed.

WHOSE HAIR WOULD YOU CHANGE ON TV?

STEPHEN: Beeny's. Frizzy bleached chunk slices.

CHRIS: We've always said that we'd like to do her hair.

STEPHEN: And she's nice, we love her. But the hair's got to go. And the three box leather jackets: one's purple, one's black and one's green. It's all she's ever got on. And she's always up the fucking duff.

CHRIS: And Simon Cowell. What's going on with that? It's a flat top with a centre parting.

STEPHEN: He's a pillock, isn't he? All the money he's got – why hasn't he got a stylist? He wears his trousers up here, his tits are down here…

CHRIS: And he wears the same clothes all the time, doesn't he?

STEPHEN: George Lamb's got great hair.

CHRIS: Beautiful hair. I've always really liked Drew Barrymore's hair.

STEPHEN: Pat Butcher. Can't go wrong with a blonde crop, can you? That's my kind of hairdressing: shit. Fuck knows how I get away with it. I used to lay tarmac before I hairdressed.

CHRIS: I'm liking Cheryl Cole's hair at the moment. Sort of rooty and blonde and all that. But how much of that's really hers? Mind you, I had implants.

STEPHEN: They took hair off his arsehole.

CHRIS: No, they didn't.

STEPHEN: You can, though. You can take hair off your arsehole and put it in your head. As long as it's yours.

CHRIS: They can take your beard hair, they can take your chest hair, or armpit hair. Anywhere. And then insert it. I don't know if, when they pull it into your head, it adapts. I mean, just imagine if someone actually had their pubes removed and put on their head.

STEPHEN: Yeah, but you could have straighteners put on it.

CHRIS:
Sarah Beeny. She's always got bumblebee stripes.

WOULD YOU NORMALLY WATCH TV TOGETHER?

CHRIS: When we were dating, we used to sit in and watch TV.

STEPHEN: Tsk. Fucking brilliant, it was.

CHRIS: Because you never wanted to go out on a Saturday night.

WHAT DO YOU DISAGREE ON ?

CHRIS: I love *Millionaire Matchmaker*.

STEPHEN: I can't stand that woman.

CHRIS: She's a bitch. But she knows her stuff. I love the fact that she really puts the millionaires in their place, because they think they're bloody God's gift. And she slaps them down, so I love her. She's great.

STEPHEN: It's a load of old drivel. I love the History Channel. And I like anything to do with World War II.

CHRIS: Oh God. Boring.

STEPHEN: Come on, you've got to love all that.

CHRIS: There's so many other things that I quite like in history, like Pompeii – anything like that is cool. *Spartacus: Blood and Sand* was very homoerotic. You're watching it literally peering through your fingers, but then you get all these full frontal naked men and you're just, like, oh my God! So you have to watch it just for that.

STEPHEN:
Mr Selfridge?
What a load of
old shit.

CHRIS:
Oh, I love
that.

GAY MEN ON TV WHEN YOU WERE GROWING UP

STEPHEN: I remember seeing Jimmy Somerville on TV and thinking, I know I'm like that, and I really don't want to be. You know, the bleached hair and the dancing like he did. It wasn't until *EastEnders*, when there was a gay couple that didn't seem stereotypical. One of them was a tall fella with grey hair.

But I didn't come out until I was about twenty-five, because I was from a council estate, and you just kept your mouth shut.

STEPH & DOM, SANDWICH

 DOM: Shooting.

 STEPH: Shopping.

REV. KATE & GRAHAM, NOTTINGHAMSHIRE

 KATE: The Suffragette movement 1897–1918. No. Forget that. *Spaced.*

 GRAHAM: The life and works of Johann Sebastian Bach. Or *Grand Designs* 1999–2003.

THE MICHAELS, BRIGHTON

 ANDREW: British politics since 1979.

 CAROLYNE: Akhenaten, the tenth pharaoh of the eighteenth dynasty of Egypt. Or the life of Elvis.

 LOUIS: The fantasy novels of David Eddings.

 ALEX: Disney Pixar films.

LEON & JUNE, LIVERPOOL

 LEON: Everton FC in the 1980s.

 JUNE: I'm not clever enough to go on *Mastermind.*

THE MOFFATTS, COUNTY DURHAM

 MARK: Newcastle United FC, 1999 to the present day.

 BETTY: Pop music of the 1980s.

 SCARLETT: Disney Pixar films.

BILL & JOSEF, CAMBRIDGE

BILL: Sloths.

JOSEF: Round 1: Cluedo (I know the inventor's daughter and have copies of the original patents and rules). Round 2 (if I get that far): Monopoly. I have copies of the original patents and also copies of the original patents for The Landlords Game 1901 and 1924 by Elizabeth Magie Phillips. Some say Charles Darrow pinched her game and renamed it – wrong! Don't get me started.

THE WOERDENWEBERS, THE WIRRAL

RALF: Football.

VIV: The Wars of the Roses.

EVE: Tattooing, or Catbug. And Jay would do video games.

THE TAPPERS, NORTH LONDON

JONATHAN: Babestation.

NIKKI: Cleaning.

JOSH: *Friends* (the TV show).

AMY: Harry Styles.

LINDA, PETE & GEORGE, CLACTON-ON-SEA

LINDA: Hairdressing.

GEORGE: Pubs.

PETE: Handing out money.

THE SIDDIQUIS, DERBY

 UMAR: *Columbo.* I know an embarrassingly great deal about it.

 BAASIT: *Batman* comic storylines from 1985. Don't judge me.

SID: Indian cinema, 1950–1970.

59

STEPHEN & CHRIS, BRIGHTON

CHRIS: Yeah. Derren Brown did this programme and he manipulated this woman to electrocute a kitten. Didn't really. It was all a bit of an illusion. It was all about making someone do something that they really didn't want to do. And this woman, she was crying, and she didn't want to push the button – and then she ended up pushing it. And there were so many complaints about that. Anything to do with animal cruelty should not be shown on TV.

REV. KATE & GRAHAM, NOTTINGHAMSHIRE

KATE: Yeah, I wrote in to complain about a sexist advert once. Do you remember the oven cleaner advert that was 'so easy even a man can do it'? I got really cross about that because it belittled men. It made men sound like they're so stupid they can't even clean an oven, which is just a ridiculous thing to say. I can't abide sexism. And it works both ways.

THE TAPPERS, NORTH LONDON

NIKKI: I nearly did. It was *EastEnders*, to do with Tanya when she had cancer. And it was awful.

AMY: They portrayed cancer in completely the wrong way. It was around the same time mum had cancer.

> **SCARLETT:**
> I tweeted Points of View saying, 'Are you going to get some young people on?'

NIKKI: Both me and my mum did have breast cancer. And at the time, me and my mum both said we were going to sit down and write to them because I was really put out by the way it was all put on. The way they portrayed the hospital thing and the chemo thing.

JOSH: They made it look as if you can only die from it.

NIKKI: It was nothing to do with that. The bottom line was the information that they were giving to the public, via the soap, was actually completely wrong. Instead of a positive thing, it was a negative thing. I'm sure they researched it enough, but whatever their research was, I didn't think it was great. I just thought, 'Hold on. This isn't right.'

 JONATHAN: Yeah, but, Nikki, that's where you've got it all wrong. People shouldn't just watch a programme and say, 'Oh, is that how it all really is?'

GEORGE:

If I have a bad meal, I pay for it and then I won't go back there any more.

 NIKKI: But people do.

 JOSH: People don't know unless they've experienced something like that.

 NIKKI: But then recently, they've done another story which has been much more factual, much better written.

 JOSH: I wrote and complained once because of a news story. It was a time where Israel and Gaza were having one of their wars and the BBC news, of course, they were being biased, but it was more that they had actual inaccurate information. So me and my friend wrote in and complained. And we got sent an email saying, 'Thank you for the complaint. We'll try and deal with it ASAP.'

LINDA, PETE & GEORGE, CLACTON-ON-SEA

 GEORGE: I don't complain about things. This is probably a very bad view to have on life, but I believe that you should not complain. You should just pay for your entertainment and then leave the premises. And I know that is probably not the best way to be.

DR WHO

THE WOERDENWEBERS, THE WIRRAL

 EVE: Something we don't agree on would be *Doctor Who*. I absolutely love it. I've got a thing about David Tennant.

 RALF: I have to watch it, because they watch it, but I am moaning. I don't get my head around it. It makes no sense for me. What's happening? I see a phone box flying around…

 VIV: It's not. It's a police box.

 EVE: It's the TARDIS!

 RALF: I see people watching really weird things…

 VIV: So uneducated!

 RALF: I think you have to grow up with it.

 EVE: He's a Time Lord! He's from Gallifrey!

 RALF: So, I start moaning and then I get in a row with my daughter because she tells me to shut up because she wants to watch it.

 EVE: I've watched it since it was brought back onto TV. But nobody in school really liked it. There was a select few of us that used to watch it. And we all got picked on.

RALF: You have to be a kid, or stoned, to understand it. Or English.

BILL & JOSEF, CAMBRIDGE

 BILL: The Daleks are still just heavy-duty waste bins with a sink plunger, aren't they?

LINDA, PETE & GEORGE, CLACTON-ON-SEA

 LINDA: Is there little midgets in them Daleks?

 PETE: What, little Oompa Loompas?

 GEORGE: If you watch *Doctor Who* and you're over the age of nine, you need to rethink your life.

DOWNTON ABBEY

THE TAPPERS, NORTH LONDON

 AMY: I know it's the olden days, but it's just so dull.

THE SIDDIQUIS, DERBY

 BAASIT: When were curtains invented? I don't know when anything was invented, you know.

 UMAR: I'd imagine they were invented after the window.

 BAASIT: I'm sure I just saw a chest of drawers from IKEA there.

THE TAPPERS, NORTH LONDON

 NIKKI: I never ever watched it when it was originally on. And then somebody bought the first series of the box set.

 JONATHAN: Yeah. Let me get my hands on them.

Steph & Dom
Sandwich

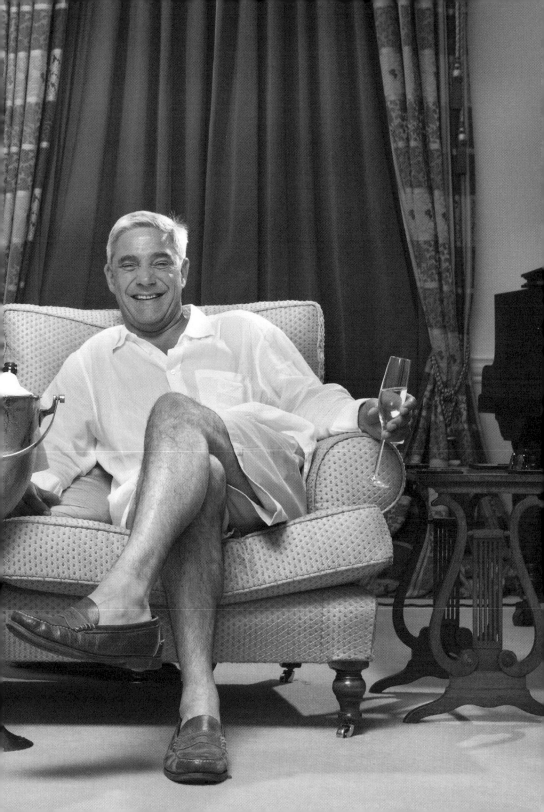

Steph & Dom

SANDWICH

———

Steph, 48, and Dom, 50, have been married
for sixteen years. They live in Kent with their
two children, Max and Honor, and their beloved
sausage dog, Gigi. Most evenings,
they crack open the drinks cabinet and settle
down to watch their favourite TV shows.

———

STEPH & DOM

HOW DID YOU MEET?

DOM: We met on a blind date about eighteen years ago. Steph was in Brussels at the time – she'd just left NATO and had gone into the private sector, and she was over for a training course. A friend of mine had been trying to get us together for about a year, and eventually I capitulated and said, 'Yeah, I'll come.'

Now, according to this chap, Steph had a thing about ginger beards. So, as he'd finally got me to drive up to London, he'd gone and bought hairy ginger hands from a joke shop, and he'd cut them out, so I had a pathetically bad, hairy, stick-on ginger goatee beard.

We get to the house. I'm in a tweed jacket with a fake ginger beard, starting to laugh. We knock on the door, and Steph answers. And I think, 'Well, that's obviously his date. Where's my date?' And I was delighted to find out that Steph was my date.

Halfway through dinner I said something about renting a house down at the New Forest – telling her a funny story about a garage door getting stuck or something – and she went, 'Oh, my God, it's you!'

And it transpired we'd met ten years before in the New Forest. I was a landlord and Steph was my tenant. I know at the time I was very interested, but very much got the cold shoulder.

And that was that. It was a done deal that night.

STEPH:

One of the questions people often ask is 'What's the secret of your relationship?' We get that an awful lot. The answer is: booze, booze and more booze.

HOW DID YOU GET ON GOGGLEBOX?

DOM: We did this programme, *Four in a Bed*. We had an absolute blast. It was really good fun. We didn't have to worry about our place, and we met some great people, and had a really good time pissing around.

And then we got a phone call saying, 'We've got this wacky idea – *Gogglebox* – would you like to come and join it?' And we said, 'Why not?' And we agreed between us that we'd do it if it was fun, and it was only four shows, and we just had a blast with it. Really good giggles. We sit on a sofa, watch telly and get pissed. I mean, you couldn't get much better than that, could you?

STEPH: It's a bit like date night for us. We have to sit and be with each other, and not get up and answer the phone, and not deal with the punters – not do anything, just sit and have a laugh with each other. So, for us, it's quite special, because we get to hang out with each other for a change.

DOM: And that's why you see us sitting holding hands, smashed on champagne and being silly.

 LAUREN D: My ideal relationship has grown from Bella and Edward when I was younger to now wanting what @stephanddom from **@C4Gogglebox** have!! #idols

WHAT DO YOU THINK OF YOURSELVES ON SCREEN?

DOM: We didn't like the first show that went out. We were all a bit unsure at the start. Also, our language is probably not the softest in the country and we felt a bit self-conscious about that. And slightly self-conscious about the fact that we were being watched in our own home. But it's just got better and better.

STEPH: I thought I was fat. I just went, 'Oh my fucking Christ! I look huge. I've got thousands of chins.' All I could do was stare at my chins. I couldn't listen to a word I was saying. I was mesmerised by this sort of moving flesh. It was vile. I know I'm not fat, but on telly I look fat, and everyone tells me I look fat on telly. But after the first series, I got over it.

DOM: I thought, 'Oh my God, I haven't got any lips. And my hair's all pokey out at the sides and looking strange. Bloody hell! I don't look like that, do I? I don't sound like that, do I?'

STEPH: You're so fucking vain now.

WHAT WAS YOUR FAMILY'S REACTION?

STEPH: Originally our family didn't like our being on telly. 'Dreadful idea! Absolutely shameful. People like us don't go on television. No, no, no, no, no.'

DOM: Oh, and 'Stop swearing.'

STEPH: 'You're potty-mouthed.'

DOM: 'Is it necessary to use the F-word all the time?' And, of course, it was just us at home alone, forgetting. So, you know, the language is free and easy. We don't care about that. Obviously, when our children are about, we try not to ... but the odd one slips in. But, you know, that's how it is round here.

STEPH: One of the questions we get asked is, 'What do your children think about it?' And funnily enough, I asked our daughter Honor on Sunday. She said, 'Well, you know, sometimes you do things that are embarrassing, but I don't really mind.' On Saturday she watches the show with me,

and there was one where we were having to review this wildlife show about walruses in a zoo – and they were trying to get mummy walrus pregnant by daddy walrus, and they were having to extract the magic juice by hand ...

DOM: Someone was wanking a walrus.

STEPH: And its tummy's wobbling away – and they cleverly blocked it out, but you could see this woman's hand going up and down. And Honor's watching, and she goes, 'Mummy ... what's wrong with it? Is it all right?' I said, out of nowhere, 'You know when you tickle a dog on its tummy and its leg goes? That's what's happening to the walrus.' 'Oh, so it's really happy?' 'Oh, yes! It's really happy!' 'Oh, that's fine, then, Mummy.'

STEPH:

Our daughter's brain wouldn't have worked out that they were w***ing off a bloody walrus... Mind you, having to explain to her what an orgy at the Gogglebox Mansion was, that was quite an interesting one.

BEING RECOGNISED

DOM: The reactions have been fabulous.

STEPH: Wonderful. People laugh as soon as they see us. They sort of point and start laughing. You can't ask for more, really.

DOM: 'We love you on the show' and 'Thank you for cheering us up'...

STEPH: There's been a lot of that.

DOM: Apart from one Scottish kid who did a rant on YouTube after we'd said something rude about the Scots. But Steph is Scottish, so we're allowed.

One of the interesting things we do is watch the show to find out who we've upset this week. I mean, at one stage I upset half of Scotland; another week I upset half of Ireland... We haven't offended the Welsh yet. But we have got to go for the full set.

We make some harsh comments about actors and actresses and presenters and things like that. But it's very easy for us to take the piss, right? It doesn't worry me very much, because I like to think that people understand it's on the basis that I don't know these people – I've never met them. I don't think anyone should take it too seriously.

I think *Gogglebox* is an amazing exercise into the world of finding out real-time, real-life points of view. And a lot of us, on occasions, are having the same reaction to a certain person or show.

Posh people probably have not had a very good press over the years...

DOM:
Interestingly, we've had a lot of people writing in to say, 'I used to hate posh people. But now we've got to know you, it's changed my whole view.'

STEPH: ...because the majority of them are arseholes. The Fucking Fulfords.

DOM: Idiots.

STEPH: And Christine and Neil Hamilton. They're just hideous. There's this sort of right to privilege that I think a lot of posh people wander around with. And it's that, obviously, that people generally hate.

WHAT DO YOU DISAGREE ON?

STEPH: He loves *Dad's Army*. I can't fucking stand it. It's so puerile and basic. Really not very clever.

DOM: *Two and a Half Men* is very clever writing.

STEPH: Can't stand it. Catherine Tate: she's great. Catherine Tate makes me change my pants. I love her. And Karl Pilkington. Fucking makes me die laughing. I'm on the floor, feet in the air, howling and howling with laughter. Dom's looking at me, going, 'What? There's nothing funny about that.'

DOM: You love awkward situations.

STEPH: Farting jokes still make me laugh. I'm forty-eight and I still find farts funny. If someone farted in my face, I would die laughing. I'd be really upset, but I'd die laughing first. I'd probably watch a channel that was just people farting. And maybe the repeat.

DOM: On +1.

STEPH: Bottoms and farts make me laugh.

DOM: But not burps.

STEPH:

Catherine Tate and Karl Pilkington: they're my Tena Lady people.

WOULD YOU NORMALLY WATCH TV TOGETHER?

DOM: Yes. We enjoy the odd rom-com movie. Steph's very much into her hospital dramas. We like the occasional period drama – *Downton Abbey*, *Lark Rise to Candleford* – and we're big fans of *Midsomer Murders*.

We do like murder mysteries: *Body of Evidence*, *Jonathan Creek*, that sort of stuff. I'm quite keen on a bit of comedy, quite like a good laugh: *Fast Show*-type things. We're not really very big on sport, the two of us. And because we've got kids, watching telly is quite a big part of our lives. But it's nice to watch what we want to watch, and not necessarily football, football, football, football, football, which is all my son wants to watch.

RAISED BY
TELEVISION

ANYTHING YOU'VE MADE YOUR KIDS WATCH?

STEPH & DOM, SANDWICH

 STEPH: *Bugsy Malone*. Love that film. Jodie Foster and Scott Baio. Lovely film.

 DOM: I thought it was childish shit.

 STEPH: And *Fame*. I thought, 'Oh, marvellous,' because I used to watch it every week. Put the DVD of the film on. My God it's rude! Effing and fucking and blinding everywhere. Leroy can't stop himself. I stopped it. I said, 'You can't watch this. Not with me sitting here.' But we did watch *Bad Grandpa*. Oh my God! He gets his knob caught in the drinks machine. Again, I like knob jokes and bollock jokes, obviously. And there's me saying I like intelligent humour…

THE MICHAELS, BRIGHTON

 ANDREW: I used to make them watch *Jason and the Argonauts* and *Clash of the Titans*: classical Greek stuff.

 ALEX: Oh my God! *Jason and the Argonauts* and *Clash of the Titans*. We absolutely love it. We used to re-enact bits.

 ANDREW: 'Children of the night – kill, kill, kill the bull…'

 CAROLYNE: We were going to call our son Jason at one point.

ANDREW:

I used to make them watch Jason and the Argonauts and Clash of the Titans: classical Greek stuff.

REV. KATE & GRAHAM, NOTTINGHAMSHIRE

 KATE: We take great pleasure in introducing our children to classics. One of the privileges of being a parent is sitting them down and going, right, we're going to watch a film together now. And the film we're going to watch is *Star Wars* or *Singin' in the Rain* or *Forrest Gump* – and you put it on and then you watch them watching it. And it's almost as good – in fact, it's better than the first time you saw it.

REALITY
TV

MADE IN CHELSEA

LEON & JUNE, LIVERPOOL

 JUNE: You never see a Chelsea Pensioner in *Made in Chelsea*, do you?

THE SIDDIQUIS, DERBY

 BAASIT: I'm sure there's a word for something like this – you know, when it's not real, but it is a *bit* real as well.

 SID: It's 'crap'.

LINDA, GEORGE & PETE, CLACTON-ON-SEA

 GEORGE: Spencer is so slippery you would not believe. He's like a corn on the cob covered in butter. He's disgusting.

 ANDREW:

He's a retard. He's got the IQ of a rabbit.

LEON & JUNE, LIVERPOOL

 JUNE: That's the first one I've ever watched from beginning to end. And it'll be the last.

JOEY ESSEX

THE WOERDENWEBERS, THE WIRRAL

 RALF: And this is someone who really annoying me: Joey Essex.

 EVE: I love him. He's adorable. I really want to meet him. I want to go and get my teeth whitened with him.

RALF: But the annoying thing about him is he is clever. Because he is stupid…and he makes money with it. When I saw him on *The Cube*, they make it really simple for him.

 EVE: 'Find the big ball, Joey. You've got to feel the balls and see which one's bigger.'

 RALF: Everyone in this room here would pick a ball, yeah, keep it in his hand, and then put another hand in the box…And then we're looking for a bigger one. But him…

 EVE: I want to go on a shopping trip with him because I'd come back looking like a twat and it'd be dead funny. I'd come back in some leopard print onesie.

 RALF: And he is a fucking millionaire. 'This is five, this is ten, this is quarter past, you know…'

 VIV: He can tell the time now.

THE MICHAELS, BRIGHTON

 LOUIS: He's probably gonna be, like, 'Oh, my nan died of a brain hemisphere.'

STEPH & DOM, SANDWICH

 STEPH: A real idiot abroad.

BILL:

Who is Joey Essex? I've heard of David Essex…

I'M A CELEBRITY, GET ME OUT OF HERE!

LINDA, PETE & GEORGE, CLACTON-ON-SEA

 PETE: I'm not eating no worms or bugs, or some bleeding kangaroo's knackers.

STEPHEN & CHRIS, BRIGHTON

 STEPHEN: But sometimes they do the trial, eat all that shit, and then the thing comes down and it's crocodile. After eating all that, you'd think they'd give them a bit of chicken, wouldn't you? Or a bit of beef? Or shepherd's pie or something?

STEPH & DOM, SANDWICH

 DOM: I'd actually love to go in the jungle, but I fundamentally wouldn't eat any of that shit. I would just be sick. So, the long and the short of it is I'd end up doing all the tasks, and everyone would stop dead, because I would refuse to eat any of that shit.

LINDA, GEORGE & PETE, CLACTON-ON-SEA

 GEORGE: Starve or fucking chuck the spider in your mouth. If you give them a week without any food, they'd eat the fucking spiders without you asking them.

JONATHAN: Kangaroo testicles aren't kosher. That's my get out.

STEPH & DOM, SANDWICH

 DOM: *QI.* We're very big on *QI.*

 STEPH: I'm not clever enough for that.

 DOM: Yes, you are.

 STEPH: Absolutely not. I'd be completely overwhelmed. *Blankety Blank,* maybe. Or *3-2-1.*

REV. KATE & GRAHAM, NOTTINGHAMSHIRE

 KATE: *The One Show.* And *Loose Women,* just because I'd like to challenge them on my feminist principles.

 GRAHAM: *Countryfile.*

 KATE: No! I'd shoot myself in the head if I had to do *Countryfile.* And the same for *Songs of Praise.* If ever I'm on *Songs of Praise* you have the right to kill me.

I hate *Songs of Praise.* It's great for people who can't get out and go to church — that's lovely, and people can have a nice singalong. But it perpetuates the myth that the church is still the same place as 1951, and it's not. Vicars don't ride around on bicycles any more in their cassocks. We've moved on.

I'd like to challenge religious broadcasting, actually. (Gosh, that's a big statement, isn't it? Flipping heck.) I'd like to see some religious broadcasting that is actually relevant and applicable and is not piecemeal — the nod to the religious budget that the BBC or whichever channel seems to have.

I mean, *Rev* is more authentic religious broadcasting than *Songs of Praise*, I would argue.

 GRAHAM: I'd be on *Grand Designs*.

 KATE: I'd like to be a zombie in *Rev*. In fact, they could do the apocalypse in *Rev*. They could actually do the day of judgement. How cool would that be?

STEPHEN & CHRIS, BRIGHTON

 CHRIS: I'd love to do something like *60 Minute Makeover*. Get bloody Peter Andre off it, because he can't even use a drill. Imagine if they brought back *Changing Rooms*. That'd be really, really good.

 STEPHEN: Yeah…I don't think I'd do that with you, because I once decorated my bedroom in five different shades of green. It was fucking vile. I'd do some sort of travel show. Try and be the next Judith Chalmers. I've got the fucking tits for it.

 CHRIS: We'd be really good at something like that Tom Daley show, where he's going round with his mate. We've been on a few holidays, haven't we? Especially the time when we were in bloody Egypt and we were on that doughnut thing…

 STEPHEN: We were on this thing that pulls you along the water and I thought I was going to fucking die. It went round and round and I shot off into the air and I was in the air long enough to think, I'm going to break my neck when I hit that water, and when I hit the water it went THUMP! And took me shorts clean off.

 CHRIS: So if we did a travel show, I'd want it to be more a cross between *An Idiot Abroad* and Bear Grylls.

 STEPHEN: *A Bare Idiot*.

LOVE LIK
THERE IS NO TOMORR
LIVE EVERY MOME

The Moffatts
County Durham

The Moffatts

The Moffatts are Mark, 48, Betty, 44, and Scarlett, 23.
Mark works as a fabricator welder and Betty manages
a shop. Their daughter Scarlett graduated from York
St John's University with a 2:1 in Sports and Teaching,
and they have one younger daughter, Eva, who is
seven. The family live in County Durham.

HOW DID YOU MEET?

BETTY: Through mutual friends. We met on a night out, but we already knew each other.

SCARLETT: They've been together since my mam was, like, eighteen, and yet they only got married last year.

BETTY: So, on our first wedding anniversary, we'd been together twenty-five years. We always were going to get married, it was just always something that we put off. Just never got round to it.

MARK: Why fix something's that not broken, I always say? The reason we got married was that the top table was getting smaller, wasn't it?

BETTY: He wanted to get married before he was completely bald. And then it was a leap year, so I said to you, 'Shall we just get married?' So we did. We didn't go on honeymoon, because we got married on 29 December, just after Christmas, so it was a straight-back-to-work-two-days-later type of thing. So, I'm still owed one.

HOW DID YOU GET ON GOGGLEBOX?

SCARLETT: Someone I know from college was working on the show. And I didn't even tell these two that I'd put ourselves forward for it. Literally a couple of hours before they came, I was like, 'Oh, what are you doing this afternoon?' She was like, 'Oh, I'm not working.' I said, 'Come home on your dinner hour because *Gogglebox* are going to come round.'

MARK: It was just dropped on us. To be honest with you, I thought, 'Ah, it's just one of Scarlett's wind-ups.'

BETTY: Me and Mark, we've watched it from the beginning. I said, 'Oh, you've got to watch this programme, it's so funny. It sounds boring, you're watching people watching TV, but it's really, really, really funny.' So when they asked us, I don't suppose we thought about it that hard. I think if I'd had weeks and weeks to think about it, I might have backed out.

SCARLETT:
He asks, 'Do you know any funny families from the north east who would fancy doing this?' I went, 'Aye, my own!'

HAD YOU BEEN ON TV BEFORE?

SCARLETT: I was on a programme on MTV, called *Beauty School*. So I knew, on TV, you need to keep talking, because they can't edit silence. So I was quite clued up, but these two were just a bit gormless.

MARK: The camera was there, and I was leaning over, to keep out of shot. Subconsciously I was, like, getting out of the way. And they kept saying, 'Look, move back in, can't you?'

WHAT WAS YOUR FAMILY'S REACTION?

BETTY: We're just ourselves. The people that know us know. My sister watches it, thinking, 'That's my sister, and my niece, and my brother-in-law.' Sometimes she'll say, 'Oh, Scarlett was picking on you last night.' But, you know, nothing new in that, really.

BEING RECOGNISED

SCARLETT: We walked out of the library after this charity night, and this man – no joke – he just pointed and went, *'Gogglebox!'* I was, like, 'That's rude!' It happens when I'm out and people are drunk, and they think they know you. We went to the Metro Centre, and people talk and talk, and then I'm, like, 'It's been ten minutes... We need to go...'

I'm like, 'Howay man, you're going to do this to every person that's talking to us, you'd never get anything done.'

SCARLETT:

If we didn't have telly, I don't know where we would see each other. Actually, it's an excuse to see each other.

WHAT DO YOU THINK
OF YOURSELVES ON SCREEN?

SCARLETT: When I saw us on telly, I wanted to hide.

BETTY: I don't wear much make-up as a rule, but for the show I took what I had off. Now I always wear my hair up and no make-up.

MARK: When I watched myself, I was, like, 'I really have no hair.' I'm contemplating shaving the lot off, you know?

SCARLETT:
Now I wear less make-up because I saw how orange I looked! I was like, 'Have they turned the contrast up on the telly?'

WOULD YOU NORMALLY WATCH
TV TOGETHER?

SCARLETT: We watch the soaps together. Well, me and Mam'll watch *EastEnders*, but he'll fall asleep. But he'll be in the room. If that counts. But we will watch anything to do with aliens and UFOs.

BETTY: These two are into conspiracy theories.

MARK: I got our Scarlett into it years ago.

SCARLETT: Anything. What was that thing we were watching? It was really good. It was about Queen Elizabeth, wasn't it?

MARK: About Queen Elizabeth I being a man.

SCARLETT: It was so interesting, honestly. It made sense, didn't it?

MARK: Our Scarlett doesn't believe we've been to the moon.

SCARLETT: Yeah. Anything to do with the moon, I get a bit obsessed.

MARK: Now I'm starting to think we have done.

SCARLETT: No.

BETTY: I don't care.

SCARLETT: I'm into conspiracy theories because I like to think that what we're being told isn't real. People think that I'm stupid because I'm, like, 'No, this isn't right.' And I think that they're stupid for just believing everything that they hear. So who's the stupid one, really?

BETTY: You can't say anything but she'll say the government's covering it up.

SCARLETT: There's a conspiracy theory for almost everything. Fluoride in the water and all that, and, like, they have a cure for cancer, but they're just not telling it because they get too much money out of all of it. I could go on for ever.

BETTY: But her ideas…

SCARLETT: I think it's even more scary to think that we're in this universe by ourselves. Like, you would like to think that there was someone else there, because it's scary to think we're all alone. But no one else sees it like that. Apart from me dad. So there you go. And me mam just sits and laughs at us when we talk about it.

MARK:
I like Bigfoot as well. I think Bigfoot's fascinating.

MARK: We heard there was a crop circle up in Shildon, so we went up there. It gives you goose bumps when you walk into one. I know it sounds a bit mad, but if you like that sort of thing, you like it. It would be boring if everybody was the same, wouldn't it?

MERMAIDS

SCARLETT: My dad made a forum about mermaids. It was really interesting.

BETTY: How sad's that?

SCARLETT: It's not sad though, mam!

BETTY: What's wrong with your head?

SCARLETT: There's nothing wrong with us. What's wrong with you?

MARK: There's loads of evidence that there is mermaids.

SCARLETT: You know, not like *Little Mermaid* mermaids.

BETTY: They've not got long hair, or shell bras, have they, Mark?

MARK: Hybrids from Atlantis or something like that. You know what I mean?

SCARLETT: They found skeletons, didn't they?

MARK: There's cave drawings in Egypt of us fighting creatures in the water. Driving spears in them.

SCARLETT: In the pyramids. And they look like mermaids.

BETTY: Everyone's going to think, 'What a load of idiots.'

DOGS: THEIR SECRET LIVES

THE SIDDIQUIS, DERBY

BAASIT: How secret can the life of a dog be? They're just stuck indoors all day, aren't they?

UMAR: The British do love their dogs like no other nation, really. I mean, the Chinese like dogs as well, but not in the same way.

LINDA, PETE & GEORGE, CLACTON-ON-SEA

GEORGE: Do you think dogs think you're mad when you're picking up their shit? They think, 'What the fuck's he doing?'

STEPHEN & CHRIS, BRIGHTON

STEPHEN: We should get a dog. You can run around like a big Mary-Anne with it.

REV. KATE & GRAHAM, NOTTINGHAMSHIRE

KATE: Everyone goes on about Buster's gonads, and Buster and his furry purse. He's five this year. Ex-racing dog. One of the great things about Twitter was that we didn't know any of his history at all. We just knew that he couldn't race, and the one time he did, he ran into the wall, that was all. And through his Twitter account, someone got in touch and said, 'They have tattoos in their ears, racing dogs.' So we gave them his number and within five minutes we'd got his parents' names, his family tree, his racing name and a photo of him as a puppy. Isn't that great? It was quite emotional. I got quite tearful. It was canine *Who Do You Think You Are?* And then all of a sudden people started messaging going, I'm your cousin, and I'm your brother, I'm your half-sister. I'm your this, I'm your that – and before long, he'd got this whole Twitter thing of his long-lost family.

His racing name was Felltop Chaos. It's quite grand really, isn't it, for Buster? We would not have called him Buster. We would have called him Heston. We like Heston Blumenthal. I'd quite like to lick his wallpaper. That's not a euphemism.

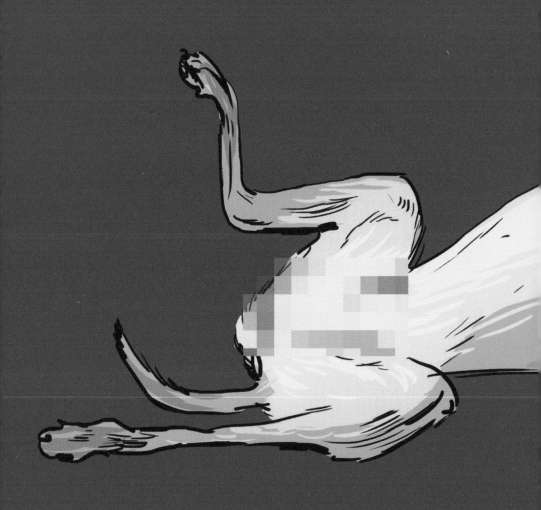

THE TAPPERS, NORTH LONDON

 JOSH: We want a dog but they won't get one.

 AMY: I want a guinea pig, but apparently it smells.

 NIKKI: The thing is about pets is the people that end up looking after it are the parents. I work full time and I couldn't have them in the house.

 AMY: Are you joking? I would look after a pet so much. It would be my baby.

LEON & JUNE, LIVERPOOL

 LEON: We're animal lovers. We had two much-loved cats, Tiger and Fudge. And I used to tell the girls stories about them. And Julie said, 'Why don't you write a story about them?' So I wrote a book: *Tiger and Fudge*. And it sold quite a few.

 JUNE: You went round schools and nurseries reading it, didn't you? We're pet-free at the moment.

 LEON: But I've asked for a kitten for Christmas.

 JUNE: And we've got the old Labrador...

 LEON: ...what?

 JUNE: You!

LEON:

The two cats used to talk to June. She denies this, though.

Tiger and Fudge
Leon Bernicoff

THE MOFFATTS, COUNTY DURHAM

 SCARLETT: We have a hamster. Called Mordecai.

 BETTY: We did have Rigby as well. Like on *Regular Show*. He's sadly gone to hamster heaven, hasn't he?

 SCARLETT: So, my dad made a coffin at work. Like when I used to have goldfish and they used to die, he'd cut the thumb off a velvet glove, put the little fishy in. He's a welder, so he made Rigby a metal coffin.

 MARK: Lined it with velvet. It's buried down the back of our veggies.

THE MICHAELS, BRIGHTON

 ALEX: I cried when you told me that my dog Sammy was still alive. We gave our grandparents Sammy to look after when their dog died, and then I kind of lived the next couple of years not really ever seeing him. And then I was told by someone that he had died; so I was really upset. But then *last week* you told me that he was still alive and I was, like, *what? My dog has been resurrected?*

NATURAL WORLD: AFRICA'S GIANT KILLERS

LEON & JUNE, LIVERPOOL

 LEON: You used to lie like that with your legs in the air, June.

SANDY & SANDRA, BRIXTON

 SANDRA: The way they eat the bones... I eat like that.

AMANDA LAMB
Very glad the vicar's crocodile slipper is covering up her dog's knob.
#Gogglebox

SUPERSIZE VS SUPERSKINNY

STEPHEN & CHRIS, BRIGHTON

 STEPHEN: Do you remember in the paper there was that big fat lady and they found a cat in one of the folds of her skin? *In the folds of her skin.* It was the next door neighbour's. They'd been searching for it for weeks and it was there, tucked in between her…gunt.

THE SIDDIQUIS, DERBY

 UMAR: Whenever I go swimming, it's the fat people who are always overtaking me.

EMBARRASSING BODIES

THE SIDDIQUIS, DERBY

 UMAR: I'll be alright as long as it's nothing to do with balls.

 SID: I think it must be hard coming to something like this and showing all your ailments and stuff, when the doctor's, like, ultra buff. I'm not saying I have a thing for Doctor Christian…

STEPHEN & CHRIS, BRIGHTON

 CHRIS: If he put a paper bag over his head I would.

STEPH & DOM, SANDWICH

 DOM: He's the doctor that does warts on your knob.

 STEPH: Look how buff he is. He's gymtastic. He's a gay icon.

 DOM: He looks like a monkey.

THE MAN WITH THE 10-STONE TESTICLE

THE MICHAELS, BRIGHTON

 CAROLYNE: Americans can send bloody ships to Mars, they can change the weather, they can…whatever it is, and they can't give their own people a health service. It's absolutely outrageous.

STEPHEN & CHRIS, BRIGHTON

 STEPHEN: Oh God. I'll never be able to eat a faggot again.

STEPH & DOM, SANDWICH

 STEPH: Life's shit, isn't it? Gives you a big bollock, takes it away, and then you die. And all he'll be remembered for is having a massive bollock.

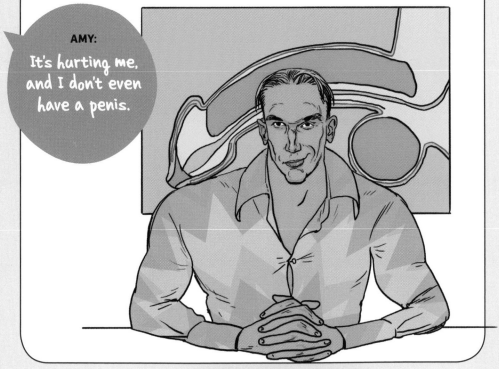

AMY:

It's hurting me, and I don't even have a penis.

Dr Christian

ONE BORN EVERY MINUTE

SANDY & SANDRA, BRIXTON

 SANDRA: My third and fourth, I said, 'No way, no – I'm not pushing out nothing. Take it out yourself.'

REV. KATE & GRAHAM, NOTTINGHAMSHIRE

 KATE: Do you remember when you had to put your scrubs on? You looked like George Clooney. Well, you did to me. But I'd had a lot of drugs.

STEPHEN & CHRIS, BRIGHTON

 STEPHEN: I've always thought women were the stronger sex. They have to put up with periods, having babies, the menopause…

 CHRIS: …Men. And they have to walk in stilettos. And that fucking hurts.

THE SIDDIQUIS, DERBY

 SID: It's an amazing feeling, when you hold your child in your own arms.

SEX BOX

THE MICHAELS, BRIGHTON

 LOUIS: Shut up, Dad! 'They should be married.' 'They can't have sex out of wedlock.' You are, literally, a thousand years old.

THE SIDDIQUIS, DERBY

 BAASIT: That box is going to stink.

BILL & JOSEF, CAMBRIDGE

 BILL: Just a note: the first European to write about the clitoris was a man called Columbus in 1516.

> **SANDRA:**
> My third and fourth. I said, 'No way, no – I'm not pushing out nothing. Take it out yourself.

LIVE FROM SPACE

SANDY & SANDRA, BRIXTON

 SANDRA: Every country in the whole world is in that ball?

 SANDY: Except the stars. The blue bits are water. We're in space, we're looking down, why isn't the water falling down from Earth?

 SANDRA: Because it ain't raining.

SHAUN RYDER ON UFOS

LEON & JUNE, LIVERPOOL

 LEON: If there are other civilisations, they should get in touch with us. Mind you, they'd probably get shot. You know how intolerant we are.

STEPH & DOM, SANDWICH

 DOM: We're going to hear of somebody telling us about the thing that came down, parked, took him upstairs, sucked him off, spat him out, kicked him back in – and it was the only way he could explain to his wife why he had a sore cock when he got home.

LINDA, PETE & GEORGE, CLACTON-ON-SEA

 GEORGE: What a load of fucking bollocks. There's definitely nothing coming in to our atmosphere from outer space. Anything that would have the technology to enter our atmosphere would be able to see everything we're doing from outside of it. They would definitely not park up and make their self known, unless they're abducting people.

UMAR:
I'd be more inclined to believe Stevie Wonder saw a UFO than Shaun Ryder.

 LINDA: What about ET?

The Michaels
Brighton

The Michaels

BRIGHTON

——

Retired hoteliers Andrew, 54, and Carolyne, 53,
have been married for twenty-eight years.
They live in Brighton with their son Louis, 17,
who hopes to be a writer. They have three other
children: Alex, 23, who works in marketing; Katy,
25, who works in recruitment; and Pascal, 20,
who is studying neuroscience at Aberdeen. When
the whole family are home, there is often a lively
debate about what's on telly.

——

HOW DID YOU MEET?

CAROLYNE: We were both doing a summer job as English Language teachers. There was a pre-arranged meeting and neither of us really wanted to go. Andy was managing his family's hotel at the time, and I think he only wanted to do the teaching so he could meet girls.

ANDREW: That's exactly why I wanted to do it. I was negotiating to buy another hotel in Bournemouth at the time and I thought, right, I've got this couple of months' window, what can I do? And I thought, well, what I'd like to do…

CAROLYNE: …is meet all these Swedish girls.

ANDREW: Yeah.

CAROLYNE: I didn't want to do it either. It was my mum that forced me to do it. At that time, every day Andy used to finish at the hotel and leave the keys for the safe in a hidden place at reception, for them to open up the next day.

ANDREW: But the night before, I had decided I wasn't going to go because it was on Sunday morning, and I thought, well, can't be bothered. I can pick up girls some other way, you know.

CAROLYNE: And then, at seven o'clock in the morning, he got this phone call from the duty manageress, waking him up to say…

ANDREW: 'The key's not here. Have you taken it home with you?' And I said, I've never taken it home with me. But I looked in the pocket of my trousers and I had taken it. And I said, oh, I have! I'll be right there with it. And I took it in and, you know, it was eight o'clock on a Sunday morning, and I thought, well, I'm up and dressed, I might as well go to the thing that I'd decided I wasn't going to go to… and that's when we met.

CAROLYNE: And you know how English people are very sort of…reserved? And if ever there's a front-row seat, nobody ever wants to sit at the front, they all go to the back? So, because I was late, all the back seats had been taken, so there was nowhere to sit except the front, and it was just me, like a Larry, sitting at the front. And, of course, because Andy was also really late, he had nowhere else to sit, so it was just us two sitting in the front like idiots.

ANDREW: And I sat there and I saw this girl with long hair. And I thought, my God, she looks good-looking: I bet when she moves her head she's going to be a right old fucking goggler. But she moved her head and, of course, she was absolutely gorgeous. And I said, 'Thank you, God.'

CAROLYNE: And the day that I met Andy, I was wearing a dress that I had *actually made myself*. And I remembered thinking, as I put it on, what's the point of looking nice? I don't care if I wear this. I'm not going to meet anybody anyway. And there you go. We were thrown together.

> **CAROLYNE:**
> Alex is named after the place we met: the Hotel Alexandra.

HOW DID YOU GET
ON GOGGLEBOX?

CAROLYNE: Katy, our eldest, was working in Hollister, and some street recruiters came in for the programme.

ANDREW: They said, 'We're looking for interesting families,' and Katy said, 'My family's really interesting.'

CAROLYNE: But when they told us what the programme was about, we just said, 'God, that's got to be the most idiotic, boring programme.' We actually didn't want to do it. Who would watch other people watching television? How could that be interesting?

LOUIS: I thought it was quite funny, actually.

ALEX:
We thought it was a shit idea.

ANDREW: I said no, it's just silly and I think there's every chance we're going to be made to look bad. But they insisted it would be fine, so I said to Louis, 'I am genuinely going to leave it to you, as a sixteen-year-old, to decide.' And he looked at me and said, 'Do you know what, Dad? Let's do it.' And that's why we did it.

LOUIS: I liked the idea.

CAROLYNE: Katy was the one who really wanted to do it – she was desperately keen. And then, literally a week before filming was due to start, she went off travelling. Just upped and left and said, 'I'm going to Australia. Bye!'

ALEX: I was in London at university for all of this, so I didn't really have a clue what was going on.

WHAT DO YOU THINK
OF YOURSELVES ON SCREEN?

CAROLYNE: At first, it was like watching a home movie. It didn't feel like it was on the telly at all.

ANDREW: It didn't feel like there were thousands of other people watching it.

CAROLYNE: Because *Gogglebox* isn't filmed in a TV studio, we're just being ourselves, so it doesn't actually feel like it is on the telly, it just feels like we're at home.

LOUIS: We don't have to go anywhere, we don't have to learn any lines…

ANDREW: We're not making an effort.

LOUIS: We're doing the most leisurely activity in the most leisurely room in our house.

CAROLYNE: We don't have to dress up; we don't put any make-up on.

LOUIS: We dress down, if anything.

HAD YOU BEEN ON TV BEFORE?

CAROLYNE: I did this makeover on *This Morning*.

ALEX: She was the hair model.

LOUIS: Basically they said, if anyone's been meaning to have a radical haircut for a while and hasn't got round to it, we're doing a competition. So, just ring us up and you might be chosen. Mum had been meaning to get her hair cut for ages because it was a bit of a state, and so she rang up and she said, 'I'd love to be involved.'

CAROLYNE: It was very radical. I hated it. But you're sitting there on the spot, and they do this big reveal, and everybody's supposed to say, 'Oh, we love it!' But it was so horrible. I absolutely hated it. I actually wanted to cry, it was so bad.

LOUIS: It was Alexandra Burke.

ALEX: An inverted bob. Dyed dark brown.

116

BEING RECOGNISED

LOUIS: It's very weird. If I'm sitting on the bus, I might catch someone looking at me. And I'll maybe assume that they might recognise me. Or I've got food on my face.

CAROLYNE:

So my idea of saving money to have my haircut was completely devastated, because then I had to go to the hairdressers and have it all restyled because it looked so shit.

CAROLYNE: People give you a double look. They really stare at you. And, to begin with, I used to think, oh my God, have I got my skirt tucked in my pants or something?

ANDREW: The bin men stopped me the other day, and one of them shouted, *'Gogglebox!'* And I said, that's right, guys. Do you like it? And he goes, 'We love it.' I said why? 'Because it's so real,' he said.

CAROLYNE: That's what everybody says. 'We absolutely love it, we love you and it's just like we sit there as a family – we're just the same as you.' My mum, unfortunately, passed away quite recently. But she was in a nursing home and all the nurses watched it, so she was absolutely made up because she felt like she was something special.

LOUIS: They gave her extra chicken.

CAROLYNE: Everybody always says how happy it makes them. That's the key. They all say it makes them happy and that's great because, for me, that is such a wonderful feeling: to think that you've made somebody laugh.

ANDREW: And they all like me, as well. Which is really weird. I'm not used to people liking me.

LOUIS: A girl messaged me, and said, 'I have been suffering from depression for a while and your positivity and your happiness is actually more helpful to me than all the drugs and psychiatric help that I've received.'

ANDREW: And what did I say to you when you told me that story?

LOUIS: That you were proud of me.

ANDREW: I did. And I meant it.

LOUIS: I think that was the first time I'd ever heard those words. That was really nice.

Andrew and Carolyne on their
wedding day, 7 June 1986

WHAT DOES TV MEAN TO YOU?

CAROLYNE: It's relaxation.

LOUIS: We can all reminisce and be nostalgic about it. Especially us four kids. We would always watch the same thing. So TV defines certain times of our childhood. In that sense, it's a catalogue.

ANDREW: Television can be unifying.

ALEX: Everybody has quite disparate lives, you know – people are off doing their thing, we're doing our thing – but when we're watching the telly, we are all part of each other's lives.

ANDREW: That's really the whole thing, isn't it? It's bonding.

CAROLYNE: And then we can talk about it. And we reminisce. We think back to all those programmes that we did sit together and really enjoy.

ANDREW: A shared history. Saying that reminds me of a friend of mine at school. He didn't have a TV. So if anyone said to him, 'Did you watch so and so?' he would say, 'No, you know I haven't got a TV.' His parents thought it would be awfully clever not to have a TV, so they could do activities. And I used to think how stupid it was. And, all these years later, I still think it's stupid.

CAROLYNE: When the children were very young I used to take them to a Steiner school. However, behind that Steiner philosophy is that you shouldn't have television. But as much as I love the whole Steiner philosophy – you know: children should be in touch with nature – I just felt I couldn't subject my children to having no TV.

I know that sounds really silly, but I had a very strong feeling that if they didn't have a television they'd be missing out on something about growing up. It's something that you can talk about. It isn't wasted time.

CAROLYNE:

I think that's why Gogglebox is so successful. Because everybody has that shared common experience.

119

FOOD AND
DRINK

THE WOERDENWEBERS, THE WIRRAL

 RALF: English people. Testicles in pies. Fucking hell, you're perverts.

SANDY & SANDRA, BRIXTON

 SANDRA: All I do is eat, eat, eat, eat, eat.

 SANDY: We all do what we do and that's what makes *Gogglebox*, because if we didn't *Gogglebox* wouldn't work.

 SANDRA: Are we the only family on *Gogglebox* that eat?

 SANDY: No, they do eat. We just eat a lot more.

 SANDRA: Yeah, pizza on the table. I love when I see a pizza.

THE TAPPERS, NORTH LONDON

 AMY: If you get a banana skin and you go like that with your banana skin to your teeth, it makes your teeth whiter because of the potassium.

LEON & JUNE, LIVERPOOL

 JUNE: The only thing I won't do is eat in front of the television. Well, you'll see us eating a cracker.

 LEON: Or a cake.

 JUNE: Leon's weight has become a bit of a running thing.

 LEON: I lost about a stone.

 JUNE: People on Twitter were saying, 'Stick with it, Leon.'

 LEON: I could do with losing another stone.

STEPH & DOM, SANDWICH

DOM: Since I was about twenty, at the end of the day – come six, six-thirty – I like something to take the edge off. A mental symbol that I'm not working any more. A drink is the mark of the end of the day. 'Right, we can, we can look to do other things now.'

My favourite after-dinner sticky would be a brandy and Benedictine. I don't have them very often because they are absolutely lethal. And I can never get the mix right. It's two of one, and one of the other, so it's a triple shot. It's just like drinking very strong nectar. Highly recommended. But if you've gone through a fairly big evening, and you have one or two of those, that's it, you're on a highway.

Bit hot and cold on gin at times.

I do a mean Bloody Mary. Absolutely mean. It's a good morning-after Bloody Mary, though. In the evenings, I don't usually go that gung-ho because it takes about forty minutes to make it.

DOM:

My drink of choice would be real ale, followed probably by red wine, probably followed by vodka and tonic. Bloody Marys are big up there.

CHRIS MULLINS

Feeling squiffy after playing a drinking game toasting every time @StephAndDomP appear on **@C4Gogglebox**

DOM'S BLOODY MARY

- A large vodka
- A splash of sweet sherry
- A splash of dry sherry
- A couple of drops of whisky
  (a peaty malt, like Connemara)
- Tomato juice
- Worcester sauce
- Tabasco
- Celery salt
- Celery seed
- Lemon juice
- Lime juice
- A tiny drop of Angostura bitters
- ½ tsp horseradish

Shake over ice and pour over
crushed ice (which has got
to melt a tiny bit first).

LINDA, PETE & GEORGE, CLACTON-ON-SEA

 GEORGE: I've never cooked anything off the telly. They won't let me. If I laid my TV on its back and started frying stuff off it, I'd get in trouble.

STEPH & DOM, SANDWICH

 DOM: I've done a couple of Nigel Slater's recipes, but his simple ones. And we've done a couple of recipes out of Jamie Oliver's books. We did a poached steak. (He poached it in red wine, naturally.) Which was great. And we ripped the recipe out of the book, thinking, 'We'll keep that safe,' and we haven't been able to find it since.

REV. KATE & GRAHAM, NOTTINGHAMSHIRE

 GRAHAM: I had a go at macaroons when I saw them on *Bake Off*.

 KATE: Graham's very domesticated.

 GRAHAM: They didn't look that good, but then I did a photo on Facebook and it was like, 'It's all right Graham, they look all right.' Tasted all right.

 KATE: I quite like coming down the stairs at night in my dressing gown and eating out of the fridge, pretending I'm Nigella. But there's not very exciting things in our fridge, usually. So I think that I look like her, but actually I just look like a fat person eating trifle.

SANDY & SANDRA, BRIXTON

 SANDRA: Sandy cooks stuff off the TV.

 SANDY: I watch any kind of cooking programme. But I experiment. Like when they say you do chicken breasts, and you put cottage cheese inside. But I noticed that when they put that in, it all comes out of the sides. It's all over the joint. So you put Philadelphia in. But not normal Philadelphia, you use the garlic and herbs. And then use your ham thing and wrap round. Such a difference. I'm a cook.

SANDRA: I'm not.

 SANDY: The way to a man's heart is through his stomach, you know that. If you can cook, your man will love you really forever. Because he knows no matter what, even if he leaves you, he knows that you're always going to be cooking. So when he's hungry he can come and find you.

I've always cooked. Because my mum used to have a restaurant. When she used to go on holidays to the Caribbean, then I used to run it. We used to have all the wrestlers in. Big Daddy's been there back in the day. It was in Brixton, Tulse Hill. Police Commissioners, people off TV, celebrities, they all used to come. Because she was one of the first Caribbean food restaurants that opened up. That's why she was known too back in the day.

THE MOFFATTS, COUNTY DURHAM

 BETTY: I don't really cook.

 SCARLETT: I've *ordered* food in after I've seen it on TV.

 BETTY: That looks nice. Order a pizza.

 SCARLETT: Whenever we watch *Man v Food*, a pizza ends up being ordered.

 BETTY: We watched one where they had to do a pizza pie, and Scarlett rang Dominos. She was saying, 'Is there any chance you could make a pizza pie?' And he was saying, 'What's that?' She went, 'It's like a pie, but it looks like a pizza… A pizza pie?'

 SCARLETT: He put us through to Head Office to see if they could help us. But they couldn't.

SCARLETT:

Whenever we watch Man v Food, a pizza ends up being ordered.

REV. KATE & GRAHAM, NOTTINGHAMSHIRE

 KATE: A nice perk of the dog collar is you very, very rarely pay for beer as a vicar.

LEON & JUNE, LIVERPOOL

 LEON: Can I have a cracker please, June? A cracker, darling.

 JUNE: No, you can't.

 LEON: Go on. You've got beautiful eyes. I'm lost when I gaze into your eyes. I always was.

REV. KATE & GRAHAM, NOTTINGHAMSHIRE

 KATE: We're so middle-class, aren't we? What's that scraping sound? It's my working-class grandfather turning in his grave. I'm going to have gravy and mushy peas for tea, just to counteract it.

 GRAHAM: Put the Prosecco away, then.

EVE: And he took Turkey Twizzlers away...

THE SIDDIQUIS, DERBY

 BAASIT: You know bananas are not actually part of the fruit food group. Fifty per cent of our DNA is the same as a banana's.

 SID: Are you two having a banana? Oh, let's get two. Banana Buddies.

LEON & JUNE, LIVERPOOL

 LEON: I'm just going to have this cracker you didn't bring me.

STEPH & DOM, SANDWICH

 DOM: Steph can't stand Nigella Lawson. More to the point, she can't stand the character – the way she's portrayed. It's all soft porn in a kitchen. And I'm sure she's not like that in real life. It's as if someone's rubbing her in places we can't see to get her to perform like that. There's a bit of frottage going on somewhere.

THE WOERDENWEBERS, THE WIRRAL

 EVE: I like Jamie Oliver's cooking, even though he ruined my school meals. I used to get my meal and I used to get my vegetables and stuff like that, and then I'd get a cookie with chocolate chips. And he replaced 'em with raisins. And he took Turkey Twizzlers away. Jay didn't like that.

 RALF: My favourite chef is Gordon Ramsay. He is my personality.

 VIV: What? Arsehole?

 RALF: Yeah.

MASTERCHEF

STEPH & DOM, SANDWICH

 DOM: Bring back the *Galloping Gourmet*. Glass of wine in one hand, one for the pot, one for me…

STEPHEN & CHRIS, BRIGHTON

 CHRIS: The thing is, these programmes, they just make you feel hungry, don't they?

 STEPHEN: Not when they're dishing up things that look like fucking shit.

STEPH & DOM, SANDWICH

 STEPH: Looks like something Gigi just deposited.

THE GREAT BRITISH BAKE OFF

STEPH & DOM, SANDWICH

STEPH: It doesn't make me want to get up and bake, I must be honest. No. Some other fucker can do it.

BAASIT:
Nothing says
'I love you'
like a banana,
does it?

LEON & JUNE, LIVERPOOL

 JUNE: Now, Mary Berry's got talent. I've got her cookery book in the kitchen. My children learnt from it. And it was well illustrated, so they knew what the dish had to look like when it was finished.

 LEON: Our Julie is a better cook than all of them. She got 98% in O-level home economics. They would have given her 100% but they said they couldn't.

THE TAPPERS, NORTH LONDON

 NIKKI: Mary Berry's old-fashioned. Old-school.

 JONATHAN: She puts a towel over sandwiches.

SANDRA:

Gregg Wallace ain't sexy like that man that cooked the bread on Bake Off.

THE SIDDIQUIS, DERBY

 UMAR: Mary Berry brings me out in a rash. We were watching *Great British Bake Off* and I had a severe reaction to something. The doctors still don't know what it was, but we maintain that it was her. 'Cause the last time we watched it something happened.

 BAASIT: Mary Berry's a curse on this family actually. Because the time before that we watched her, they couldn't use any of our footage because something went wrong with the camera.

 UMAR: And the time before that we had a power cut, I'm sure she was on it then. I don't know. She's... I think she's evil in some respects. I think she's undead.

 SID: I was going to say she resembles a modern-day witch.

 UMAR: Yes, you're right. She's one of them white witches.

 BAASIT: She can hear us now. You've got to stay quiet about this.

THE MICHAELS, BRIGHTON

 CAROLYNE: How is Mary Berry so thin when she cooks all those cakes? It's not fair. If I could be like her and grow to be that age and be doing what she can do, I'd be well impressed with myself. She's the same age as Elvis.

SANDY & SANDRA, BRIXTON

 SANDRA: Yeah, I like her. I would love to live like her right now. Tea and cake.

 SANDY: And scones. Or sc-oh-nes.

 SANDRA: And everyone coming round for a cup of tea in the garden, sitting down. Yeah. That's the kind of life I would like to have.

 SANDY: And nowadays people don't cook and eat like they used to. And these younger generations, they don't know how to bake one cake, much less a Victoria sandwich. Unless they learn it once in a year in school. I mean, I can't bake. But I watch her.

STEPH & DOM, SANDWICH

 DOM: Sweet old poppet.

 STEPH: She is a Victoria sponge.

STEPHEN & CHRIS, BRIGHTON

CHRIS: She comes across as a sweet old lady, but I think she's a right dirty bitch.

The Siddiquis
Derbu

The Siddiquis

DERBY

———

The Siddiquis are Sid, 69, an environmental
manager for the NHS, and his sons Umar, 36,
a biomedical scientist, and Baasit, 32,
a teacher. Sid and his wife also have two
daughters and a third son, Raza, who appears in
the show occasionally. They live in Derby.

———

HOW DID YOU MEET?

UMAR: We're family, obviously, but we lived together for a considerable period of our life. *Gogglebox* is just an extension of how we talk and interact with each other anyway, it's just that somebody's put a camera there.

BAASIT: What comes across as genuine is the fact that we haven't just been thrown together for the purposes of this programme. We do know each other very well.

SID: My son Raza did all of the first series alongside Baasit and Umar. He's quite hilarious. He's deadpan and the opposite of me. If I say it's day outside, he'll say, 'No, it's night.' That is pretty good because then it gives a chance for us to react to each other, whereas these two, they usually tend to agree with me. But Raza is very, very much, in your face – 'No, Dad, you're talking rubbish.'

BAASIT: Dad used to lie to us. When we were very young, and then a bit older, but a bit thick. Dad used to tell us that he wrote *EastEnders* or *Coronation Street*, and he knew what was happening next.

SID: Because I'd read the magazines.

BAASIT: We used to believe him as well. We were idiots.

UMAR: Dad told me that he'd been on *This is Your Life*. And just presented us with a generic red leather-bound book as the proof.

BAASIT: We never got to look in it, did we?

UMAR:
Dad told me that he'd been on This is Your Life. And just presented us with a generic red leather-bound book as the proof.

137

Sid when he was 25 years old, 1974

Baasit when he was
14 years old, 1994

Raza (8) and Umar (9)
in their school uniforms,
and Baasit (4), 1986

HOW DID YOU GET ON GOGGLEBOX?

BAASIT: I have a friend who I used to work with in a video shop years ago. She went off to uni and then I just carried on with my life, and then she just randomly sent me an email, out of the blue, and said, 'You're a bit of a prat, we're doing this thing that you might be interested in.' I said I'd ask Dad and my brothers and see if they wanted to give it a go. And they jumped at the idea. But none of us thought it was going to be on Channel 4 or anything like that.

SID: We thought, it's only a small thing, nobody's going to even notice, we're not going to become celebrities or anything like that. So that was the perception at that time. But when the second series came, things changed quite a bit, and obviously the third series is just crazy. It's enormous.

BAASIT:
I'm really bad for putting my hands between my legs. It's horrible.

WHAT DO YOU THINK
OF YOURSELVES ON SCREEN?

SID: It's unnerving. 'Why do I look like that? Why am I sitting like that? Look at my stomach sticking out. Oh, I shouldn't be doing that.' I've got this terrible habit of folding my arms.

Ours isn't a posh image at all. You only have to look when they show the outside of the house: the bins are stacked up there. It's a funny thing, because I went to a work conference, and we go round the table to introduce ourselves, and when my turn came and I said, 'I'm Sid Siddiqui', somebody else shouted 'Get those bloody bins out of the scenes.'

UMAR: It is shocking though, isn't it? When they do the pan of the house and you can just see wheelie bins. And then they show the posh couple's house...

BAASIT: On Twitter, the most negative thing that anyone said about us was that we don't have necks.

UMAR: I think it's because we all sit like this.

BAASIT: You should change your sofa, man, seriously.

WHAT WAS YOUR FAMILY'S REACTION?

SID: My wife wouldn't want to be on the show. I mean, she's not fluent in English anyway, so that would be a problem.

BAASIT: Mum and the sisters... I think they're our worst critics. In fact, I think it's one of them who Tweeted that we have no necks.

BEING RECOGNISED

BAASIT: It's weird. You can go through your day-to-day life just absolutely normal: I go to work, I get yelled at by my boss and the kids pick on me and stuff. And then you'd go out in town, when all three of us are together... it's like Power Rangers. So many people start crowding you.

BAASIT: And they don't call you 'The Siddiquis', they call you 'Gogglebox'.

SID: Actually, people are very kind and respectful. They recognise you, but they don't want to intrude.

BAASIT: But when people have had a few drinks, then they feel like they can just ask anything.

UMAR: When I get approached I'm a bit embarrassed still. I would like to continue to be a bit embarrassed.

141

WHAT'S YOUR
TV GUILTY
PLEASURE?

THE WOERDENWEBERS, THE WIRRAL

 RALF: I love the American shows, with police chases. How stupid people are. Because if the helicopter is over you, you know there is no escape. I would stay. I would brake and say, 'Yeah, OK.' It's like these people are sitting in jail and they don't know why, because they think they do nothing wrong. That is, for me, like, 'Wow!' My strawberries in the fridge have more brain! You know what I mean?

THE MOFFATTS, COUNTY DURHAM

 BETTY: Anything on TLC, I watch. *Mob Wives.*

 SCARLETT: I love it, I follow them all on Twitter.

 BETTY: *Toddlers and Tiaras* I love. It's this American programme on TLC, and it's literally kids in pageants. And it's like child abuse watching them. They're two, and they wax their eyebrows.

 SCARLETT: This one girl had a Madonna outfit and she had, like, the cone bra, she had a spray tan.

 MARK: It's just so wrong on so many levels.

 BETTY: It's wrong, but you watch it and you can't believe it. And most of the kids don't even really want to do it. It's their parents who are saying, 'We'll do it. You're enjoying it…' They're all mad Americans, spending thousands and thousands and thousands for every pageant.

LEON & JUNE, LIVERPOOL

 JUNE: Gok Wan. He was so lovely and gentle and polite. What a really nice person. I saw him in John Lewis once.

The other thing is Gareth Malone and the choir. Love that. We watched that from when it first started.

SCARLETT:
Actually, I watch it, and it makes me want to make my little sister do it.

145

THE SIDDIQUIS, DERBY

 BAASIT: My guilty pleasure is *Made in Chelsea*, and I know I shouldn't like it. I try to watch it with Mel, my wife, and then she gets tired and goes up to bed and I'm thinking, I'm a guy, I can't sit here by myself watching *Made in Chelsea*, this is just wrong… I'll just watch another fifteen minutes.

 UMAR: Me, living on my own, I've got what would be described as unusual taste in programmes. I don't really watch anything post-1999. It's all very old shows. So *Columbo*, *Quincy*, *Jeeves and Wooster*, really old stuff. I'm just stuck in the past. But some of those things are quite good as well.

STEPHEN & CHRIS,
BRIGHTON

 STEPHEN: *Judge Judy.*

 CHRIS: God, it's awful.

 STEPHEN: I just love her. She's mental. And really, it's the same case every time. It's either 'You smashed my car' or 'We moved in together, then you moved out and you've got my VCR'. That's all it is. But I just love her responses. She's this old Jewish battle-axe, but she's really good at her job. She just wants facts and then she makes her decision. It makes me laugh. But it is crap.

STEPH & DOM, SANDWICH

 STEPH: *I'm a Celebrity…Get Me Out of Here!* I just love Ant and Dec.

 DOM: *BGT* and *The X Factor*. And we sort of enjoy *The Voice*. But then, when you get to the end of *The Voice* it becomes either a *BGT* or an *X Factor*, because they've seen the face. And actually, you should probably not see the face at any stage.

 STEPH: They should do it all behind a screen.

 DOM: That's not such a bad idea, you know. Funnily enough, just thinking back to that apparent masked orgy (we weren't here, we don't know) that's pretty much going to have sex with a bag over your head. It's probably about the only time these people get to have sex, because nobody knows what they look like.

BILL & JOSEF, CAMBRIDGE

 JOSEF: *Prisoner Cell Block H.* I found myself being drawn to watching it, simply because I thought it couldn't get any worse. And every week it seemed to. It was like a school play. Ridiculous. Crass nonsense. I've forgotten how or why I started watching it.

THE MICHAELS, BRIGHTON

 CAROLYNE: *Escape to the Country.* That's on in the middle of the day, when you really should be doing other things.

THE TAPPERS, NORTH LONDON

 JOSH: *Homes under the Hammer*, and *Location, Location, Location*.

 NIKKI: He's obsessed with property.

 JOSH: It's not like what house they're buying, or they should buy that one. I just like seeing the houses. I prefer Phil to Kirstie, though.

 AMY: I watch hair and make-up tutorials on YouTube. 'Hey, so today I'm gonna be showing you how to roll your hair…' I wake up in the morning and I come downstairs, and watch a bit of TV before I go to school.

 JONATHAN: In the morning, it's *Babestation* daytime.

 AMY: And I turn on the TV and go into the TV guide and find *Babestation's* been recorded at two o'clock in the morning so they're fully naked. I just delete it.

LINDA, PETE & GEORGE, CLACTON-ON-SEA

 GEORGE: I really love BBC4. I had an awkward moment when I got deeply involved in the Drake equation the other day. You know, the one they have for working out if there's alien life. I watch and then I start Googling shit. I'm on my tablet, looking up everything. I go on 'Safari' and I'm looking up the double slit experiment, and then I'm off looking up something else. It's powerful. You know, Schrödinger's cat, is it alive or dead? And so on.

I'm reading about that at the moment, but I haven't got to the end yet. No spoilers. I didn't do that stuff at school. They were still counting in quarters and eighths. I got to about the age of twenty-six and thought to myself, I've got to learn something. So I watch an enormous amount of National Geographic and Discovery. So, like Ricky Gervais said, I know a lot about Nazis and sharks.

REV. KATE & GRAHAM, NOTTINGHAMSHIRE

 KATE: A fish-finger sandwich on white bread with a smear of mushy peas on it and *I'm a Celebrity…Get Me Out of Here!* And a cup of tea.

 GRAHAM: I've got a guilty secret late at night.

 KATE: I've caught you watching it. You dirty boy. And it wasn't sex. I would've been happier if it'd been *Sexcetera*, but it wasn't.

 GRAHAM: *Mighty Ships.*

 KATE: One night, I could hear the telly on. I thought, what's he doing still up? I came down in my dressing gown and walked in and he turned it off really quickly. He looked like a guilty man. I thought he was watching porn. He wasn't. He was watching an engineering programme about ships.

 GRAHAM: The best one was about a cable-laying ship; they laid this cable across from Norway to England or something. And it was incredible what they were doing, welding these things together, going for miles and miles. And it had to be dead on, you know. Four miles down they got a little joystick and they were, like, 'Oh, I'm just about in the box now, there's two millimetres.' It was very exciting.

 KATE: And I have to sleep with this man.

JONATHAN:

Is Babestation a guilty pleasure? The women are not as nice as they used to be any more. They're getting older as well.

REV. KATE & GRAHAM, NOTTINGHAMSHIRE

 KATE: Quiz shows with questionable formats and rules that you can't understand. It's always some hairdresser from Burnley and they always wheel them out and it's some easy question and then they've just won £1,000 and you've got no idea how they got there. I've got GCSEs and A-Levels and degrees and I don't understand it. I like my quiz shows like I like my men – simple, and straightforward. And not too many flashing lights. And big knobs.

STEPHEN & CHRIS, BRIGHTON

 CHRIS: That whole judging panel thing. Too much of that. Everything's got fucking four judges.

 STEPHEN: *Masterchef.* You can't even follow the recipes, because they don't tell you them, do they?

 CHRIS: And they're just such miserable bastards as well. All they do is shout at each other. Oh – and I don't want to watch adverts for fanny pads.

 STEPHEN: Vagiclean or something.

 CHRIS: Yeah, for thrush and stuff.

 STEPHEN: Women know they've got to clean their minge. They don't need an advert about it, do they?

 CHRIS: And it's always when you're eating.

 STEPHEN: There's something about the word 'vag'.

DOM:

An hour and a half of Crufts would kill anybody.

ZOMBIES

THE MOFFATTS, COUNTY DURHAM

 SCARLETT: The thing I don't get about *The Walking Dead* is who cuts the grass?

REV. KATE & GRAHAM, NOTTINGHAMSHIRE

 KATE: We like lots of the same movies. We both like a good body count.

 GRAHAM: Tarantino. And you like zombie movies.

 KATE: I love a zombie movie.

 GRAHAM: Every time we go to somewhere new, like on holiday or a town or a shopping centre, Kate's always going, 'Well this would be a great place if there's a zombie apocalypse because you could go in there…' She works out a sensible place to hold out.

KATE: I can't believe you *don't*. Whenever we go anywhere new, it's my first thought: how will I survive a zombie apocalypse here? Why wouldn't that be your first thought?

 GRAHAM: What'll happen to Buster in the event of a zombie apocalypse?

 KATE: Well, he'll get eaten eventually.

REV. KATE:

Obviously, they'll leave Buster's most famous bits 'til last. Save them for when someone says, 'I'm a zombie, get me out of here,' and then we'll make zombie Ant and zombie Dec eat them.

HARRY POTTER

STEPHEN & CHRIS, BRIGHTON

 STEPHEN: Emma Watson – she don't come off the estate, does she?

LINDA, PETE & GEORGE, CLACTON-ON-SEA

 LINDA: I always wanted you to be Harry Potter, George. Because I wanted you to fly.

STEPHEN & CHRIS, BRIGHTON

 STEPHEN: You watch: give it a couple of years, old Radcliffe will have blown all his money on drink and hookers. He'll be phoning up old JK Rowling – she'll be in an old people's home stinking of piss – going, 'Go on, write another one, me career's on the skids, I'm skint, bring Harry back…' and he'll do a Harry when he's about thirty-five.

TITANIC

STEPH & DOM, SANDWICH

 DOM: OK, so it's 1912, Jack's twenty years old, Rose's stark naked – tell me he hasn't just jizzed in his pants.

LEON & JUNE, LIVERPOOL

 LEON: If you love somebody it's everything, isn't it? I'm crying, June.

GHOST

REV. KATE & GRAHAM, NOTTINGHAMSHIRE

 KATE: She's up in the middle of the night making pots. Most people get up and watch Family Guy.

THE WOERDENWEBERS, THE WIRRAL

 RALF: They're forming a cock together.

LEON & JUNE, LIVERPOOL

 LEON: If you were sitting like that, June, I wouldn't bother with the pottery.

LINDA, PETE & GEORGE, CLACTON-ON-SEA

 GEORGE: He's a right goer, he is. I'd never last until the end of the record.

AMY:
Did the Titanic actually happen?

NIKKI:
Yes, you silly cow.

Rev. Kate & Graham
Nottinghamshire

Rev. Kate & Graham

NOTTINGHAMSHIRE

———

Reverend Kate Bottley, 39, and her husband Graham, 46, live in Nottinghamshire. Kate is the vicar of three churches and Graham, a vicar's son, is a violin teacher. They have two children, Ruby and Arthur, and a greyhound called Buster, whose undercarriage has become something of a star in its own right.

———

HOW DID YOU MEET?

KATE: Ah, it's a lovely story, how we met. I first saw Graham at school. I was about thirteen or so.

GRAHAM: And I was a loser trying to retake my A-Levels.

KATE: I saw him running across the quad for his violin lesson. I remember it very well. And I said to my friend, 'Who's that?' And she said, 'That's the vicar's son'. And I thought, 'Better get my arse to church.'

GRAHAM: So it's my fault you're a vicar?

KATE: I went to church for a snog and ended up with a dog collar. It wasn't quite my intention. I was twenty-three and Graham was twenty-nine when we got married. And my dad's, like, a steel-working footballer kind of thing – and I bring home *a violin teacher who's a vicar's son*. My dad took me into the kitchen and went, 'Is he right, hen?' I went, 'Yeah, he's fine, Dad. Don't worry. It'll be all right.'

HOW DID YOU GET ON GOGGLEBOX?

KATE: They found me because they wanted a vicar. And I did a flash mob at a wedding that went viral on YouTube. I do between twenty and thirty weddings a year, and the weddings here have gone from just a few a year to a massive number – partly because I'm The Vicar That Likes To Say Yes as much I possibly can. So, when someone says, 'Can we get married at your church?' the answer is always yes.

And I always say to them, if you want to personalise your wedding, just ask. And this particular bride and groom, they'd been waiting for their wedding day for a long time, you know, and she wanted something very different. She wanted it to be a wedding to remember. So she said to me, 'What's your craziest idea?'

REV. KATE:

They found me because they wanted a vicar. I did a flash mob at a wedding that went viral on YouTube.

HOW DID YOU GET ON GOGGLEBOX?
(continued)

And I said, 'Well, I've always wanted to do a flash mob.'

Now, flash mobs are early noughties, rather than right now. But the Church of England is always a healthy twenty years behind everybody else. Next thing I know, she's booked eight weeks of rehearsals. She sent me the video of it, because I couldn't get to all the rehearsals (because they were on Sundays), and it was 'Everybody Dance Now' by C&C Music Factory, and 'Celebration' by Kool & The Gang.

And we did this flash mob. I don't need any encouragement to be over the top, so, as it was coming to an end, the bride went, 'Go on, Bottley!' Well, I'm a massive hip hop fan. So I just went into Running Man down the aisle. And while they were on honeymoon, they posted it on YouTube so their friends could see it, and it got 25,000 hits in twelve hours. And I think it's got two million hits now.

REV. KATE:

I'm a massive hip hop fan. So I just went into Running Man down the aisle.

HAVE YOU BEEN ON TV BEFORE?

KATE: Channel 5 asked me to do a pilot which was based on the cartoon *Wacky Races*. They wanted to get cars and teams of drivers themed around professions; so the hairdressers would be racing in a giant hairdryer-shaped car, and the farmers would be racing in a giant sheep-shaped car, and the dentists would be racing in a giant tooth-shaped car, and the vicars would be racing in a giant church-shaped car. And I was so close to saying yes, just for the laugh.

GRAHAM: I hadn't been on TV.

KATE: I'd been doing little bits and bobs of media for years and years and years, and Graham goes straight in with a double BAFTA nominated 4.5 million on a Friday night. I've been trawling *Calendar* and local stations for years. Git.

WHAT DO YOU THINK OF YOURSELVES ON SCREEN?

GRAHAM: Well, the first time it was very weird. The first time we were actually shaking on the couch.

KATE: And I wasn't scared on my wedding day! Our bits don't seem real. It feels like *only we* see our bits and nobody else is watching our bits. It's only when you go out you realise. I was in London last Saturday, and people stopped me on the tube to take pictures and ask me if it was me and stuff, and you think, shit, people watch it.

GRAHAM: Three million people a week.

KATE: I had TweetDeck for a while, and if anybody tweeted anything about '*Gogglebox* vicar,' I saw it coming in. But I've turned that off because it all got a bit too much. But there were some *very funny* exchanges.

There was one that said, 'Oh my God, I can't believe how much I hate the *Gogglebox* vicar.' And then his mate had come in and said, 'I know what you mean, with her dirty pig trotters up on her husband's lap, the fat bitch. I bet she stinks too.' So I waded in – because I just can't help myself – and went, 'Thank you so much for your feedback.' At which point, the guy went, 'I'm going to burn in hell, aren't I?' So I went back in and said, 'Don't worry. God is very forgiving (me not so much).' And he put,

'Keep up the good work #sorry.' And I put, 'Don't worry, my feet really are a bit whiffy.' And then he followed me. So did Gaby Roslin. She wanted to know about Buster's willy.

> **REV. KATE:**
> Colin Montgomerie started following me on Twitter the other day. That was a bit weird.

GRAHAM: It did get a bit dodgy, though, didn't it, with the gay marriage issue?

KATE: Yeah, yeah. But I expected it. The Archdeacon phoned up and he said, 'Kate, we've had a letter in.' And I went, *just one?* Well, that's not *bad*, is it? I expected far more than one. And he said, 'The person was very concerned about you saying that you're pro equal marriage. Now, I watched the show on Friday, Kate, and I didn't hear you say that you're pro equal marriage.' At which point I said to him, 'Oh, I'm so sorry, Archdeacon, did I not make it clear?'

I said, don't worry, I know I'm not allowed to do them and I won't do them until I am allowed to do them, so I'm not going to break the law, because organisations are far better with people like me *in them* than being sacked from them. So I won't break the law. Of course I won't. And I won't enter into a same sex marriage myself, because that's what the rules say. I'm not divorcing you to marry a woman, Graham.

GRAHAM: Oh. All right.

The downstairs loo at
Rev. Kate and Graham's

WHAT TV DON'T YOU AGREE ON?

KATE: I don't like Kevin McCloud. Graham loves Kevin McCloud. He's got a bromance boy crush on Kevin McCloud.

GRAHAM: He's my hero.

KATE: Graham would leave me for Kevin McCloud and his over-budget-ness. He buys *Grand Designs* magazine every month. He's got all the DVDs.

GRAHAM: I haven't got *all* the DVDs. Only the first few.

KATE: I feel like I've lost my husband when there's a new series of *Grand Designs* on. I have a little *Grand Designs* bingo card. You get extra points if Kevin speaks in a foreign language. It's the only way I can get through the show. Unless I did a Kevin McCloud drinking game. Graham's got this idea…

GRAHAM: *Grand Designs*: *The Opera*. There's so many little stories you could go down. Two houses being built on stage, and stuff.

KATE: This: this is his vision.

GRAHAM: Kevin McCloud trained as an operatic tenor, you know.

KATE: It's the same show every week! All they do is change the names to protect the innocent. It always goes over budget; they've always got pretentious names; she's always the bloody project manager and is *crap* at it; the glass never arrives on time; and she always ends up pregnant. More money than bloody sense, the lot of them. And then Kevin thinks it's a triumph. Every single time. 'It's a triumph.' Oh, shut up, you smug arse.

168

DO YOU HAVE A PARTY TRICK?

KATE: I can get my whole fist in my mouth. I found that out when I used to play rugby. You find out all sorts of things about yourself when you play ladies' rugby. I also found out that I could down a pint in about three and a half seconds. Not really useful. (Except when you're finishing off the wine at communion. Because the rule is that once you've blessed the wine, you have to finish the wine.)

I do three services on a Sunday morning: eight o'clock, half nine, eleven. Once, I did the three services, everything's fine. Went to finish the wine and it hit my stomach. And I don't know what it was, but I suddenly felt *that's not stopping there*. So I said to the person assisting me, if you just announce the next hymn, round things off, I'll be back in a minute. Went to the loo, threw up like a good 'un, felt so much better. Don't know what it was. Came back, everything was good. Until I realised that I'd still got my microphone on. But because the congregation had been singing 'Bread Of Heaven', it was OK, because it just gets louder and louder in the chorus.

And we're both jugglers. He taught me to juggle. One of my cunning ways to get him to put his arms round me.

REV. KATE:
And I can eat fire.

WHAT DOES TV MEAN TO YOU?

KATE: There's a slight sniffiness about TV. Middle-class people going, 'Oh, well we don't watch much television,' like it's something to be proud of. And I just think that's ridiculous. It's our culture. *It's our medium.* It's *how we communicate.* It's what we do. So to go, 'Oh, well, actually we just spend all our time listening to Radio 4 and reading Nietzsche,' you know ... get a life, for goodness' sake. Everybody else is doing it.

SANDY & SANDRA, BRIXTON

SANDY: *Alien.*

SANDRA: Yeah. *Alien.* Because I dream a lot, you know. If I watch anything too tough, I dream about it in another version.

SANDY: Yeah, she takes it to the extreme. Like you'll get it at one stage on the TV, like somebody will be biting their neck. But in her sleep, they'll be biting it and chopping off her head. She takes it to the next level.

LEON & JUNE, LIVERPOOL

JUNE: I don't like anything where it's very, very dark and enclosed, because I'm claustrophobic. I have had terrible nightmares over things.

THE WOERDENWEBERS, THE WIRRAL

VIV: Eve wanted to watch *A Clockwork Orange.* And I wouldn't let her so she went somewhere and watched it. She was too young for it. And *The Exorcist.*

EVE: You let me watch that on my fourteenth birthday, and you came in and I was laughing at it. You thought I'd be under the bed. When her head was spinning round, I was *howling*, it was so funny.

 VIV: It's a really weird thing, but before Eve was born, I used to watch horror films. And I didn't mind how horrible, because I used to be a veterinary nurse, so I wasn't bothered about blood and guts and cutting things up. But after she was born, I just didn't want to watch horror films. I think when you become a mother, you become more protective and you think, 'Oh my God, people do these kinds of things.'

THE TAPPERS, NORTH LONDON

 JOSH: You tried to stop me watching *The Bill*. Mum was like, 'If you're getting nightmares, Josh, you should stop watching *The Bill*.' But I couldn't help it. It was so addictive. I had to watch it every week.

 JONATHAN: The thing that I watched that terrified me was *The Exorcist*.

 AMY: Oh my God, we watched it the other day. I could not stop laughing. I think it's the most hilarious thing. If I had to categorise it, I would say it was a comedy.

 JONATHAN: Hold on. I was *nine* when I saw it.

 JOSH: The Child Catcher in *Chitty Chitty Bang Bang*.

 NIKKI: That used to petrify me. And the witches in *The Wizard of Oz*.

 AMY: Dad used to be scared of tractors.

STEPHEN & CHRIS, BRIGHTON

 STEPHEN: *Crimewatch* can be a bit scary, especially if you watch it and you've got to get all the lights out and then run upstairs and get in bed.

THE MOFFATTS, COUNTY DURHAM

 SCARLETT: *Crimewatch*. I love horrors, but it's *Crimewatch*. Like, honest to God, I go to my room and push me bed up against the door because I've watched *Crimewatch*. Every noise that I hear, it's like, 'Oh my God!'

 BETTY: So, if somebody breaks in, it's all right if they slaughter the rest of your family, as long as you're OK?

THE SIDDIQUIS, DERBY

 BAASIT: *The Ring*. When the girl crawls out of the TV. It's because everything looks like it's ending in that show. And I was just sitting there, going, 'It's just like *X-Files*, this, just a bit of a mystery, they've solved it.' And then *that bit* happens. And it just messed me up so much. Because I thought, what's she going to do? She's going to get up near the TV, show her scary face... And then she starts walking through the TV! Ugh, God! Because you trust TVs, don't you? I had a TV in my bedroom, and after that film, it always looked a little bit brighter when it was off. And I was like, 'Shit! Something's going to happen.'

 UMAR: I remember a while ago, the BBC did this documentary called *Ghost Watch*. I think I was at school, maybe twelve years old. That really upset me, watching that, because it was the way that it was done. And they called the ghost Pipes, because he made the pipes rattle, but we used to live in a house where the central heating used to make noises.

BAASIT: Dad did this dodgy central heating.

 SID: Don't bring me into this.

 BAASIT: I was on the phone to the exorcist. 'Our house is haunted!'

STEPH & DOM, SANDWICH

 DOM: When I was about twelve, I saw this film, *Dracula AD 1972*. I was really sucked in. It was so real and so modern that I believed it was all really going on. That *really* frightened me. I didn't sleep for two or three nights after that.

 STEPH: I love being scared, because I quite like extreme emotions. I was watching *The Conjuring* the other night. It freaked me out. I was on my own. The girl in it is lying in her bed and then something pulls her by her leg – and that's my childhood fear, right there: that something under my bed will come up and grab me. I had to turn it off. Went downstairs for a smoke. Came back up, panting. I was alone in the house. And hearing every noise: every sound. Everything. *I absolutely shat myself.* And then the next night: bang, on it goes. More! I wanted more!

BILL & JOSEF, CAMBRIDGE

 JOSEF: I was watching a film on television late at night, and there was a big storm outside. I've forgotten what the film was, but it was about this couple who bought a house which was haunted, and there's a big storm, and the lights flicker three or four times, and eventually the ghost forces them out the house and they sell it on to someone else, and you see the new owners going in and the lights flicker and flash like mad, and that's the end of the film. And this storm was raging outside. And I thought, 'Cor – that was quite a good film.' And the lights all flickered and flashed, and the lightning started, and I thought, 'Shit…'

 BILL: When I was about seven or eight, there was a serial of *Dr Jekyll and Mr Hyde* being shown on ITV. I was alone in the house watching the first episode, and it got to the moment when Jekyll had taken the potion, and then it broke for the adverts. And the last advert was for Potter's Catarrh pastilles and it ended with a ditty that went, 'Stop that cold before it starts/ Act without delay/Pop a Potter's in your mouth/And drive the germs away... germs away... germs away...' And then, as the 'germs away' was fading, Mr Hyde came and flashed up on the screen going 'Aaarrrggghhh!' And I was absolutely terrified. Totally jumped. I had a phobia of Potter's Catarrh pastilles for ages after that.

THE MICHAELS, BRIGHTON

 LOUIS: *Jeopardy*. It was a CBBC drama about this group of kids that got lost on a school trip in the outback, and they all got separated. And then it turned out that they were all getting abducted. If your eyes turned red then you were going to get abducted. Everyone was talking about it. If you didn't watch the last week's episode you were not worth being friends with. It was so good. And that was terrifying.

 ALEX: I didn't find it scary.

 CAROLYNE: Was there anything scarier than the Power Rangers when you were younger? The monsters were horrific.

 LOUIS: God. The budget was so low, the scariest thing was the attempt at CGI.

> **CAROLYNE:**
> The Power Rangers scared me.

LINDA, PETE & GEORGE, CLACTON-ON-SEA

 PETE: When I was about three, I've never forgot it. It was *The Genie and the Lamp*. I can remember hiding behind me mother's armchair.

 GEORGE: The scariest thing that I've ever seen is when, on *I'm a Celebrity*, someone got put in a fucking bowl of eels. Like a snake thing. Water snakes. I can't stand them. I can't remember who it was, but I don't think he came out. You know, Pete'd be fine on that. I can see him, standing at the top, scooping them out, putting them in jelly.

The Woerdenwebers
The Wirral

The Woerdenwebers

THE WIRRAL

—

The Woerdenwebers are self-declared rock god and rock chick Ralf and Viv, 51 and 52. They live with Viv's drama student daughter Eve, 20, who is going out with Jay, 21. They live in The Wirral in Cheshire. Ralf is the drummer in the band Civilian Zen and works for Bosch. Viv runs a new age and alternative shop. Eve is about to start her own tattooing business, while Jay helps out in Viv's shop.

—

HOW DID YOU MEET?

RALF: We met in a really drunk, drunk, drunk, drunk...

VIV: He always says this and it makes me look in a really bad light.

RALF: We were both drunk.

VIV: My friend and I used to go to a place called the Hotel California, in Birkenhead. It's a really big old pub, and they can have live music all night because there's no houses around. It was 22 December and we weren't going to go because it was Yule and we're pagan, and we usually have a party with the Yule log burning and everything, and all our friends round. But we were having such a good time in the Hotel Cali, and we were dancing to 'Du Hast' by Rammstein, and drinking Jägerbombs. And my friend came back from the loo and she shouts, 'He's German! Him down there!' And he was standing with his friend. So I went to him and I said, 'What does "Du Hast" mean? Does it mean "you hate"? Or what?' He said, 'Well, you can say it two different ways.'

RALF: It has two different meanings.

VIV: And then we started talking.

RALF: I was in Hotel California with my friend from my band. We had done a CD and it was finished, so we get out to celebrate it, because it's months and months of work. I'd come to see a Who tribute band, but it was absolute rubbish. But the interesting part of it is, when you start a CD you look for a name. And my band didn't know that we were going on the show *Gogglebox*. And you know what the CD is called? Tell Lie Vision.

VIV:
We were dancing to 'Du Hast' by Rammstein, and drinking Jägerbombs.

HOW DID YOU GET ON GOGGLEBOX?

EVE: Basically, my mum owns a shop in Birkenhead Market, so we were just doing our thing in there and a woman walked in from Channel 4. 'One of your friends has said you'd be good on this thing where you watch telly, and give your opinions on it.' And we were like, 'Yeah, OK then.'

VIV: You wanted to do it, didn't you? Because Eve's at university, doing drama. So she wanted to see the other side, and she said, 'Oh, can we do it? Can we do it?'

EVE: I didn't jump right at it. I spoke to me mum, and Jay was there as well. So we had a bit of a discussion about it and then we were like, 'Yeah, all right then.'

EVE:
we didn't think it was going to be as big as this, so that's another shock.

WOULD YOU NORMALLY WATCH TV TOGETHER?

VIV: We do sit round together and watch the telly.

RALF: So when the meal is done, Vivien calls and says, 'The meal is ready.' The other two come down and then we watch TV all together, for an hour or two. Sometimes only an hour because Eve has stress from the uni, and she has to do work.

EVE: We do all love *NCIS*.

VIV: We've got really into it because we watched it from the beginning. The characters have really progressed, they're really different, but they're all like a family. That's what I like about it, that they all look after each other.

EVE: Ralf is definitely Gibbs.

VIV: Yeah, Ralf is Gibbs. Jay's McGee. Eve, you'd be Abby.

HAD YOU BEEN ON TV BEFORE?

RALF: I was on TV in Germany with my band, people running around my drum kit with cameras, you know? I was on television when I was a kid. In the Karl May Festspiele Elspe. I played, like, a little Indian boy. We did all the stunts. We had a stuntman, and he'd come and teach us. I jumped from fifty metres into water at the end of the show, with a big bomb going up, and everything explodes. I started when I was six years old, and did it for seven years.

EVE: Jay's more worried about the way his hair looks.

WHAT DO YOU THINK
OF YOURSELVES ON SCREEN?

EVE: I can tell you how she felt: 'Oh, oh, I look awful, oh!'

VIV: 'She' is the cat's mother, thank you very much. No, I get mortified. I hate watching myself.

EVE: Close-up of you eating a YumYum.

VIV: But that's what you do, isn't it? In real life, I'd sit here eating a YumYum.

EVE: Not as polite though. We eat very polite on camera. I'm like … knife, fork, napkin.

VIV: I always drop it down my top.

EVE: And Ralf has it round his face.

RALF: If I sit here and eat how I eat in a restaurant, it would not be real.

EVE: Can I point out, though: we don't eat takeaway all the time. But because the crew is set up in the kitchen, there's no way for us to cook anything. Mum and Ralf are chefs, so we don't eat shite.

VIV: I've put a stone and a half on since we started filming. I weighed myself and was like 'Oh my God!'

EVE: I looked at a photo of myself after we'd finished filming last December, and I look like I've stuffed food into my cheeks. I'm a hamster.

BEING RECOGNISED

RALF: Like last night on the airport, on the border, I give my passport. She looks and says, 'You're on *Gogglebox*.' And I say, 'Is it a crime?' People see us as Ozzy Osbourne's family.

VIV: I used to watch *The Osbournes* all the time; it was a really funny show.

There was some review in a magazine, and it called us 'the goth family', and it said 'they look as if they've spent all their life listening to Black Sabbath tribute bands over a pub in Wolverhampton'. And I was thinking, 'We're from The Wirral'.

RALF: Maybe there is one thing we can get clear in the book...

VIV: That you're German?

RALF: No. That I don't go in to the pub to watch cover bands. I am in the band. I see it this way. I play in a rock band, so when I play gigs, after the song, the audience clap their hands. So here you're doing really dry stuff, and you don't see your audience, do you? So the 'clap your hands' for me, it's when people are saying, 'Oh, that's Ralf. Can we make a photo? I really like the show. I really like you.'

EVE: It's a nice feeling.

RALF: Sometimes.

EVE: I've not been really one for attention. I'm not that into it. I don't think that we let it go to our heads, do we? I'm not like, 'Oh, yes, I'm on TV. Look at me...' Jay likes it.

RALF: I've never had someone say shit. You?

EVE: No.

VIV: The end of the market is a service road, and a lot of people drive past and they shout 'Gogglebox!' out of the car window. I'm like, 'Yeah, OK,' and I wave.

RALF: When viewers are making pictures with me, if they say, 'Is it scripted?', I make a joke. I say, 'No. Because I can only speak English. I can't read.'

> **EVE:**
> I got free chicken bites the other day. The guy at the shop said, 'You're the local celebrities, aren't you?'

SILENT JAY

VIV: People say he's not allowed to speak, and he looks as if he's being held hostage or something.

RALF: Some people were saying that he's my son, and he can't speak English, and this is why he doesn't talk.

VIV: I know some people have said that they think he's a mass murderer or a serial killer because of some of the looks he gives us. They said, 'You're going to see him there one day with a dripping knife or something and them all lying there.'

EVE: That or incest. We had a couple of girls the other week, they saw us holding hands, and they were going 'urgh' at us because they think that we're brother and sister. You know, because it's a family show. But we're boyfriend and girlfriend.

RALF: Because he is this character now who doesn't speak, I can tell you, when he speaks, Twitter will explode. But it makes it interesting.

If you've seen *EastEnders* or *Coronation Street* or series like this, they end always in a drama, so you want to see the next one. And now, with his character, that he has created for himself. You know, people are watching the next show, going on Twitter, before the show starts, 'Will he speak tonight?' But I think when the time does come, Jay, you will have to go absolutely berserk about something. You know, standing up, and hitting the hand on the front of the telly, screaming at the telly and saying, 'You absolute dickhead!' or something. 'I have had enough now!'

EVE: It's obvious he's not a murderer. The *Gogglebox* people do CRB checks and everything.

RALF: They check if you have paid your TV licence.

FLEET STREET FOX: Best things about #Gogglebox: 1) the vicar's dog 2) Silent Jay. One day, one of them will pass comment. It's the only reason I watch. Frankly my money's on the dog speaking first. **#Gogglebox**

TIM LOVEJOY: With a touch of the hair Jay says so much **#Gogglebox**

SILENT JAY:

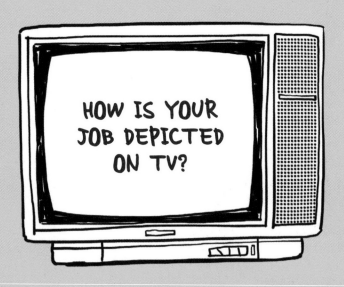

THE MICHAELS, BRIGHTON

Andrew and Carolyne used to be hoteliers.

 ANDREW: *Fawlty Towers* was touching a raw nerve.

 CAROLYNE: There were a lot of similarities.

 ANDREW: Like, one bloke we had, he had a room overlooking Bournemouth Bay and he had a big double door to the balcony. He was complaining because there wasn't enough fresh air coming into the room. I said, well, you've got double doors you can open to the maximum. You get plenty of air in. And he said, 'No, no, I want more.' And I said, well, you know, the only way we can do it is if we open the two other windows at the side: if you really want, I'll get the maintenance guy to open them right up. I thought this was bound to be a solution to get even more air into the room, because it was a hot day.

And he said, 'No, no, no, that's totally unacceptable.' At this point I was a bit pissed off. I said, well, why is that unacceptable? He said, 'Because the seagulls will come in and frighten my wife.'

And you remember Nobo boards, with the little individual plastic letters? Well, every night we had a different film we'd advertise on the board. And there was one time there was a very old lady celebrating at the hotel.

So I got to put up...

> **ANDREW:**
> Fawlty Towers was too realistic to be funny...

> **CAROLYNE:**
> It was a bit worrying, wasn't it?

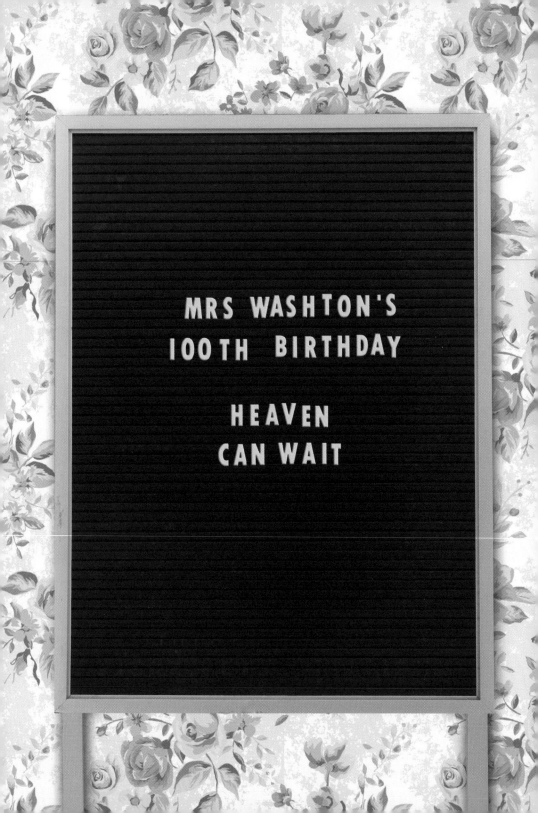

Jonathan used to be a restaurateur. Nikki works in a nursery school.

 JONATHAN: I love Gordon Ramsay.

 JOSH: *Gordon Ramsay's Effing Kitchen Nightmares.*

 JONATHAN: I can relate. I did run a restaurant. Originally it was a family business, which was started by my great grandparents in 1920, called Bloom's. A kosher restaurant. There was one in Aldgate, one in the East End and one in Golders Green. My place wasn't Gordon Ramsay's type of dining, where you have a group of chefs. What we had were cooks as opposed to chefs. There weren't really any new dishes. It was just the traditional dishes that have been going for years and year and years. It was passed down.

 AMY: Apart from Spaghetti Bolognese.

 JOSH: That was my idea. To put that on the menu.

 JONATHAN: But Ramsay's programme was always far-fetched. The thing about those programmes is they're very predictable. They always start the same way, and pretty much always end the same way, with a happy ending: it's the last night and he gets it really, really busy. There was a couple where he walked off, and gave up on them because they were impossible.

 NIKKI: I'm a nursery teacher, so I love watching those *Supernanny*-type programmes. There's nothing the parents don't know. It's just taking control of the situation and making your mind up. And you see these kids having these tantrums. I mean, it's not rocket science, is it?

NIKKI:

It's much easier when it's other people's children.

LINDA, PETE & GEORGE, CLACTON-ON-SEA

Linda and Pete used to run a pub.

 PETE: You see people running pubs on TV, and you think, 'Yeah, that's right, he's got it right.' And, 'No, he ain't got it.' I tell you, Al Murray: he can run a pub.

 LINDA: You need *characters* in a pub.

 PETE: I tried to do bleeding rolls once. Great big things, they were. Like logs. The pensioners used to wait there all night 'til we give them away. But we had this bench and all the old boys used to sit round the Public Bar. We called it 'Death Row'. And they'd be all sitting there. And you'd say, 'Old Decker's died, you'd better move along the seat, then, hadn't you? Your turn next.'

 GEORGE: We grew up in pubs. I was forty-one when I was eight, you know what I mean? I still go into the pub and drink J2O, and I sit there. Because that's my living room.

> **PETE:**
> For my money, the least convincing pub on telly is the one in *Emmerdale*. Because they never have any bother.

LEON & JUNE, LIVERPOOL

Leon and June used to be teachers.

 LEON: We liked *Educating Yorkshire*, didn't we? When the blonde girl turned and said, 'Cheeky bitch,' that was brilliant.

 JUNE: What shows in *Educating Yorkshire* is the dedication of a lot of teachers, and particularly the one with the boy with the stammer. I did teach a boy with a stammer once and I know you have to be patient and you have to deal with the others in the class. Because there's always somebody ready to be silly. 'I'll be the class clown this afternoon. Who can I pick on? Oh, I'll pick on him because he can't answer back quickly.'

Teachers are having a terrible time at the moment. Sanctions have been taken away; there's more and more pressure on them. It's sixteen years now since I taught, and the last stint I did was because somebody was off sick. Leon came down at ten past one in the morning and said to me, 'What on earth are you doing? Are you marking?' And I said, no, I've finished the marking and now I'm doing the check lists of their achievements and so on. And I thought, in the old days, I'd have finished my marking and I would have been preparing. I just wonder how teachers do it all these days, I really do.

Educating Yorkshire does show the positive side: how children can change and how they're all individual and they're not all going to get As. These targets and league tables really make me angry. League tables... Anybody would think it was the football pools.

 LEON: I don't like... what's the one on BBC1?

 JUNE: *Waterloo Road.*

 LEON: *Waterloo Road.* I don't like that. Improbable situations.

 JUNE: And too much going on in the staff room for my liking.

THE SIDDIQUIS, DERBY

Baasit is a teacher. Umar works in a lab. Sid is an engineer.

 BAASIT: As a teacher, I think that Jack Whitehall's show gets it really wrong. I can't believe they make something like that. The relationship he has with the pupils. I know that it's a comedy and they're trying to blow it out of all proportion, but it's just ridiculous. It was just trying to get laughs through shock value and inappropriateness. There wasn't anything clever about it really.

But with *Educating Yorkshire*, I think that was a more real account of what a school is like. As opposed to *Educating Essex.* There were some teachers on there that just looked like they were playing up for the camera a bit too much. And *Waterloo Road.* You just sit there and you just shake your head and you go, 'It's nothing like that.'

SID: My particular interest is in space and science and technology, because I do come from that background. I was watching something the other day, about how they created the flexible foundations for these tall buildings which are susceptible to earthquakes. And it was an amazing concept, a vacuum being used to hold two cups together and you can never take them apart. We've done that sort of thing on *Gogglebox*. When you suck a glass up to your face and you can't dislodge it because of the vacuum in there. We turned *Gogglebox* into a science documentary. And we showed the planetary system, with food.

> **JOSEF:**
> I watch the news, and when it comes to things which I know about, such as tax, I get quite incensed.

 BAASIT: You used an orange and I ate the moon mid-demonstration.

 UMAR: I find it funny, the misrepresentation of my job on TV, because I work in a lab. In any kind of hospital drama, it's one lab doing all the tests for the entire hospital and you'll have a doctor in there, running up and doing his own tests, which I know full well does not happen.

 BAASIT: Can you eat sandwiches in your lab as well? I've seen that. Where they're just casually eating sandwiches in a microbiological lab.

BILL & JOSEF, CAMBRIDGE

Bill is a writer and Josef is an accountant.

 JOSEF: I watch the news, and when it comes to things which I know about, such as tax, I get quite incensed. I think to myself, you haven't even given a *tenth* of the information. But I do understand: if they gave the whole information, the news would last about five days. And people still wouldn't understand at the end of it.

BILL: There's this recent trend to have Professors for the Public Understanding of Science. I've often thought that, probably from the moment quantum theory was invented, there has been *no hope* for the public to understand science. What we want is a Professor for the Public Misunderstanding of Science. Brian Cox is a Professor for the Public Gross Oversimplification of Science. And he does it very well.

REV. KATE & GRAHAM, NOTTINGHAMSHIRE

Kate is a vicar. Graham is a violin teacher.

KATE: TV vicars. Well, it's Geraldine from *The Vicar of Dibley*, isn't it? Hasn't done us any harm as female clergy because people automatically think you're going to be nice. They also automatically think you're going to like chocolate, which is not my thing. (I prefer a good Stilton and a nice glass of port, to be fair.)

But people already think you're going to be nice because the only girl vicar they know is the *Dibley* one. And even though it's been a long time since they did *Dibley*, it's still very much in the public conscience. I thought it was just because I'm short and round that people go, 'Oh, you're *just* like the vicar of Dibley,' but no, the tall skinny girl vicars get it as well.

GRAHAM: There's the bumbling vicar in *Four Weddings and a Funeral*. And that one in *Gavin and Stacey* who ends up shouting the Lord's Prayer at everybody.

KATE: But also vicars on things like *EastEnders* and *Emmerdale* aren't always painted in the warmest and kindest of lights. I love *Rev.* I cry a lot at it. Especially when, say, he wants to chuck it all in, and then the next minute Colin walks in and lights a candle or something — all over the country there are vicars sobbing, going, that's me, I'm such a bad person, I'm just trying my best. Graham, what do you think about the depiction of violin teachers on TV?

GRAHAM: Absolutely shocking.

WHAT TV
MAKES YOU
LEAVE
THE ROOM?

EVE: *Dogging Tales* disgusted me. I was just, like, 'No, you're all dirty bastards.'

 RALF: So Eve walked out. To sit on the stairs.

 EVE: Ralf, he perked up when I left.

 VIV: I was shocked that Channel 4 made a programme like that.

 EVE: I'm glad I couldn't hear it properly.

THE MICHAELS, BRIGHTON

 ANDREW: *The X Factor.*

 CAROLYNE: *The X Factor.*

 LOUIS: Or, when *Friends* used to be on…

 ALEX: *Friends!* Oh my God. *Friends.*

 LOUIS: Whenever *Friends* would come on and the theme tune would play, Dad would come into the room and change it.

 CAROLYNE: 'Not fucking *Friends* again.'

 ANDREW: Probably once.

 LOUIS: Oh God, no –

 ALEX: Dad, you hated it.

 LOUIS: We weren't allowed to watch it.

 ANDREW: That's true in the early days, when you were very young…

CAROLYNE:
We never, ever watch the Queen's speech.

ANDREW:
We don't do monarchy.

 CAROLYNE: ...because there's a lot of sex in *Friends*.

 ANDREW: Constant references to casual sex.

 LOUIS: We would turn it over and you'd turn it back.

 ALEX: Mum watched it, and then got me into it, and I think I was obsessed with *Friends* from the ages of about twelve to eighteen.

LINDA, PETE & GEORGE, CLACTON-ON-SEA

 LINDA: Jim Davidson.

 PETE: Oh yeah. I walked out of a theatre with him in it. I don't mind effing and blinding, because I can match anybody, but I find him so personal with people. He's a self-opinionated flash bastard. You do what you like, but I see these old girls getting offended, and I don't particularly like you too much.

LEON:
Celebrity Masterchef.

SANDRA:
I don't do babies coming out.

Sandy & Sandra
Brixton

Sandy & Sandra

BRIXTON

—

Sandy, 48, and Sandra, 52, have been best
friends for more than forty years. They live
in Brixton, the area which gave Sandra her
nickname 'Queen B'. Sandy has a background
in bar management, and Sandra looks after her
youngest grandchild five days a week.

—

HOW DID YOU MEET?

SANDRA: I've known Sandy forty-odd years. I knew her mother.

SANDY: My mum used to own a club back in the old days. Everybody used to come to my mum's place.

SANDRA: She's a club family woman, and I'm the one that goes and spends the money in the club.

SANDY: Sandra is very well known in Brixton. So for promotion and anything, we just phone her up and say, 'Get the peeps.' I had two wine bars and one pub.

SANDRA: My third child — I met the father at a party in her mum's place. And that's twenty-seven years ago. We're close.

SANDY: If she's in a mood, nobody can talk to her. There's only one person.

SANDRA: If anyone pisses me off, yeah?

SANDY: If anybody, yeah, gets on her nerves, and she's on one, I give them a piece of my mind.

SANDRA: And everyone's got respect for both of us. But sometimes people want to take the piss, and they won't take the piss when she's around. She don't put up with

rubbish or shit. And let me tell you something about Sandy as well: the last year and a half of my life, I'm putting her in stitches of laughter. She's my fan. And I'm her fan.

> **SANDY:**
> Sandra is the one who brings the people in.

SANDY: We don't argue much, except I'm more of a person to be wild. I'll go camping and stuff like that.

SANDRA: She'll say, 'We're going to the moon,' or 'We've got to go and live in the bushes,' and I end up going, 'No, I'm staying in Brixton.'

SANDY: So when I say this, she'll argue with me. She'll say, 'Why are you going there for? You don't need to be going to these places.'

SANDRA: I get scared of the news sometimes.

SANDY: Like that plane going missing.

SANDRA: Well, I'm not flying now. Because yesterday on the news, there's another plane with the wing hanging off. I watch the news every morning. I'm up at six o'clock. And I've always got to be up early because I've got my kids. I'm a full-time babysitter from Tuesday to Friday, lying there with a two-year-old. I'm a full-time grandma and a celebrity.

HOW DID YOU MEET? (continued)

Like the Queen Mum. You get me? I'm fifty-two years old, I've got a routine. I watch *Emmerdale*, *EastEnders*. So my phone is locked off between seven and nine. Plus, I've got my eating hours, my boyfriend hours, my children hours. That's how my life is. Also, in the future, I want to run seven boyfriends, if I get some money. But if they're all on JSA, I might have to give them a fiver each. £35. One to rub my toes. One to rub my knee. My belly. My arm... you know what I mean? I'm going for it, you know? You think I'm doing this for the fun? I'm heading for Hollywood. On that road... I want to go to Hollywood.

SANDY: You'd have to fly.

SANDRA: Yeah, but someone said there's a Chinaman's trying to dig a tunnel there.

SANDRA:

She'll say, 'We're going to the moon,' or 'We've got to go and live in the bushes,' and I end up going, 'No, I'm staying in Brixton.'

HOW DID YOU GET ON GOGGLEBOX?

SANDRA: It was my fifty-first birthday party. I was in my local pub where I've been drinking every week for the last ten years. Sandy did have her old pub at that time in Peckham – like, a private all-nighter that she's got a licence for – but I was in my evening pub. So it's me and Sandy, celebrating my birthday. She's left her own pub to come and sit down in my Brixton pub, which she does regularly when she wants fun, because her pub's kind of sophisticated.

So anyway, I went to the bar. They all know me, because my name's Queen B and the pub's called 'The Beehive'. So I came back with the drinks, and the next minute this man came over, a white guy with this piece of paper, and he says to me, 'Is your name Queen B?' Apparently they've decided to come in the pub to look for somebody in Brixton to go on this programme, and the barman's said, 'That woman over there, that's Queen B, talk to her.' So he came to me and goes, 'Give me your number and we'll get back to you.' And days later, they rang me and said, 'Would you like to come and do it?' So I rang Sandy, and I go, 'Sandy, they're coming up. Get ready.'

SANDY: I didn't think about it. Because we're doing exactly the same thing as this anyway on a normal day.

SANDRA: And oh, we had a lovely time. Food! Payment! Luckily Sandy was leaving her pub, because she would have had to if she wasn't. Because it turns out this is a full-time job that she never knew she was going to get. It was perfect timing, because if she'd never come, who else would I have got to do it? Because she's my best friend.

SWEARING

SANDRA: When she lets off on *Gogglebox*, you can hear it, you know what I mean? We're shocked sometimes when the producers let it go through. Because it's not everything that goes through.

SANDY: Especially sometimes because we're Caribbean and our swearing is completely different from English. Someone not from Jamaica might say 'fuck off' or 'piss off', but we say 'raasclaat', 'bumbaclaat'. It's really swearing and I don't swear like, ever.

SANDRA: No, the Grand National, she does.

SANDY: Yeah. I swear right through the Grand National.

SANDRA: And that's what black people do.

SANDY: If you go to the bookie's office that's what they do.

WHAT DO YOU THINK
OF YOURSELVES ON SCREEN?

SANDY: We cracked up, didn't we? I love watching us.

SANDRA: I'm so busy because I'm a full-time grandma, so I didn't watch it 'til Wednesday in my daughter's house. And I watched, and you know what? I'm proud of myself.

SANDY: I was in stitches. I'd phone her or text her on the phone from my house. And I say, 'Turn it on now. Turn it on now. Wait for that bit to come up.'

SANDRA: They're always up in her face.

I've always got my long nails. I get them specially done in a shop. Two weeks ago, I had my nails done for watching TV, so it's due today. But on my last week on *Gogglebox*, I was moving house, I didn't need the nails. But you think I can go on national TV with no nails on? So I'm doing these stick-on ones, with glue.

SANDY:

If you watch it they're always up my nose or in my eyes. Yeah, they love doing close-ups of me.

WHAT WAS YOUR
FAMILY'S REACTION?

SANDY: My family love it. I've got two kids, and my youngest one, she's going to uni. She's doing law, and she says in college and everywhere she goes, they're proud of her. All her teachers: 'That's your mum?'

BEING RECOGNISED

SANDRA: Because I'm well known anyway, in Brixton, we're not kind of fazed about being famous. And being the only black people on it, it kind of brings us out a bit more. Sandy got free tickets to go and see *Thriller* on stage. Cut the story short, we went there early, seven o'clock, they said, 'Come back in half an hour.' We thought we were going in the normal audience. When we came out of the toilets, security come over and say, 'Hello… excuse me, ladies? Are you from *Gogglebox*? Can you come this way, please?' And they took us in the box! You know where the Queen sits, upstairs?

SANDY: One of the royal boxes.

SANDRA: And she's, like, 'We want champagne, send me some up.' Because she's used to all this. Sandy and me, we're both two different people. I like a pub, she likes a club.

SANDY: Wine bars.

SANDRA: So we got into the box and we're sitting there...

SANDY: ...and instead of them watching the show, they were pointing up to us.

SANDRA: Fucking hell! Oh listen, you don't know how it feels. I went all shy.

SANDRA: So we were watching *Thriller*, and my heart's beating because I get overwhelmed through anything. I kept on saying, 'Sandy, where are we? What's going on?' Because I'm still in shock. And you know the monsters in the show? They come in, when I'm up there, in the dark. One of them comes in! Into the box!

SANDY: Yeah, one came in to see you.

SANDRA: So I was screaming over the balcony.

SANDY: That was mad.

SANDRA: I was screaming, and he was all in bandages.

SANDY: And the people were singing to you, the guys. And we got rushed in Leicester Square before that too. By the massive picture house. We were together, and we couldn't move. They wouldn't let us go. People from everywhere. Every nationality came that day. It was like when somebody does a book signing and people queue up.

SANDRA: Yeah, I've got that going on now.

SANDY: But we don't go on Twitter while the programme's on.

SANDRA: When I am on Twitter, I play I Spy With My Little Eye. I just talk and play games with people. Normal conversations, you get me? And no one has said nothing wrong. One person said something bad. One. And that was my son's friend. He must have tweeted my son, and said, 'Oh, your mum's talking too much.' I just said to him, 'Come off my page. Now.' And he did.

SANDRA:
We don't say no. We never say no.

211

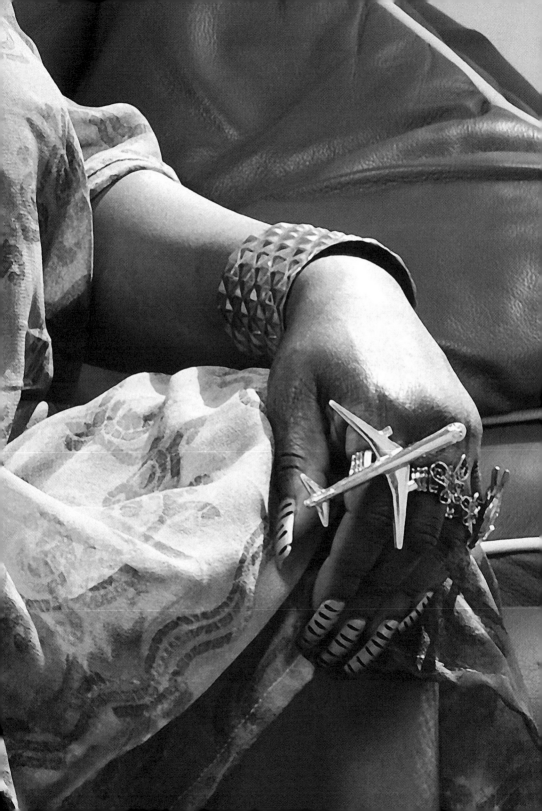

WOULD YOU NORMALLY WATCH TV TOGETHER?

SANDRA: Yes, *EastEnders. Wendy Williams.* Some African programmes.

SANDY: We watch everything. We're TV addicts. And when you're watching, you don't sit there and say nothing to each other. That's rubbish. Any family has something wrong with them if you all just sit there all silent, not even saying nothing.

SANDRA: One time, we were filming and the door was shut and one of the lights blew. Do you think anyone came in to help? They left us in here. And when I was playing with my whip, watching *Chatty Man*, doing Britney Spears. And I took the whip and it went in my face. An accident. It fucking hurt. And they filmed it.

SANDY: Things do happen, which is funny. Things which are unexpected. It's not planned. It's not us doing it. It's like when there was the rat.

I was sat here, and he came out and looked at me from over there. But it was filmed and it was excellent. It worked. You know it went into somebody's handbag.

ANYTHING YOUR PARENTS WOULDN'T
LET YOU WATCH?

SANDY: Dirty films. I mean, nothing really came on TV back then. Maybe a one-off tit or something.

SANDRA: We never got what is going on today.

SANDY: But then my mum wouldn't allow us in the front room anyway to watch television. They always had a key and locked it, so we didn't really get to watch TV. Not unless it was a day when my mum was in a good mood and she might give us, like, an hour or two to come and sit in the front room to be quiet. You know: West Indian families. Queen B's Dominican, but I'm from Jamaican parents.

SANDRA: I grew up with a lot of family. Everybody was in each other's houses. Lots of kids, lots of families, too many people.

SANDY: Yeah, we had that. But my mum was very stern. Because you're talking about seven girls and two boys. So she had to be, like, *proper on*. You get away with murder now. I didn't get my first TV until I left home. Remember? You couldn't answer no home phone.

SANDRA: We had a padlock on it, on the phone. So you had to rattle it to make a call.

SANDY: Yeah. Rattle the button at the top.

SANDRA: We had a phone box. And my mum made sure I paid, God bless her soul. When I first got my Giro, it was £11 a week. I was about fifteen or sixteen. And my mum took five and left me with six. I'll never forget it. And that is the truth.

POT NOODLE

SANDRA: I always use the Pot Noodle pots to drink out of. I had millions before, but then I threw them all away. I had a collection with lots in there.

SANDY: You had a Jerk Chicken one.

SANDRA: I use the pots. It's big, instead of having a little small cup. When I drink, I drink big.

SANDRA: Yeah, chicken and mushroom. Listen. Don't get it twisted, you know. Everyone who watches the show keeps on saying, on Twitter, 'Where's the aeroplane? Where's the Pot Noodle?' You know, if they can't see them. Guess what I said. 'It's in a vault. A Channel 4 vault.'

THE SIDDIQUIS, DERBY

 BAASIT: The *Big Bang Theory*. It's intelligent comedy, but the main characters are idiots. And that's what's so funny about something like *Frasier*. He's a psychiatrist, they're well-to-do, but this stuff is very slapstick and silly.

 SID: I like Frasier's pains that he goes through, his pains about everything in life.

 UMAR: Bit of a sadist really, aren't you?

 SID: Yeah. I miss Tommy Cooper. And Morecambe and Wise as well. I think they were really good.

 BAASIT: *Fawlty Towers.*

 UMAR: *The Fall and Rise of Reginald Perrin.*

 SID: But the funny thing is, that sort of comedy's not popular now, is it? Because Elton John had a go, didn't he?

 UMAR: Ben Elton.

 SID: It didn't look right at all, and he wrote it in the similar style as they used to do it.

 BAASIT: *Only Fools and Horses* is hard to watch now.

BILL & JOSEF, CAMBRIDGE

 JOSEF: I hated *Monty Python*. What a load of rubbish. But I liked *The Goons*. I think *The Goons* were really funny. I like *Fawlty Towers*. They changed the name of the hotel every week. There's one – how they got away with it, I don't know – Flowery Twats.

 BILL: Wasn't it a pity that Nigel Farage didn't stand in Newark? Because Newark's an anagram of 'wanker'. (And 'William Hartston' is an anagram of 'It thrills a woman'.)

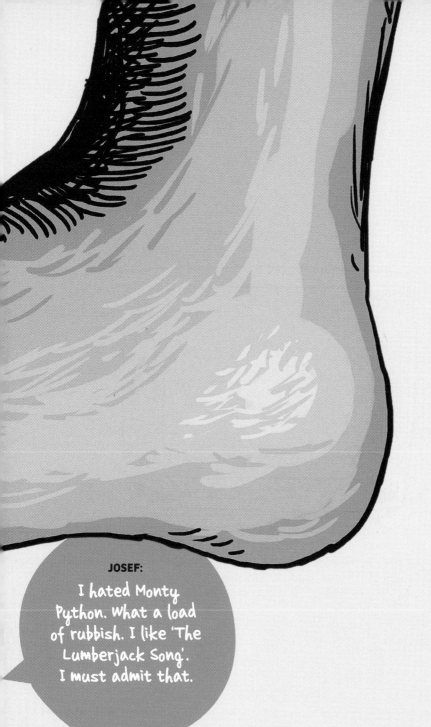

CAROLYNE: We worship at the altar of Jon Snow.

 ANDREW: An absolute gentleman. And thank God for the most impartial news on British TV, Channel 4 News. We watch it every dinnertime, without fail.

 CAROLYNE: Religiously.

 LOUIS: We're not allowed to have anything else on.

 CAROLYNE: There was a piece where Jon Snow had been interviewing Russell Brand, and then Krishnan Guru-Murthy said, 'A man who looked like God interviewing a man who looked like Jesus Christ.' Which was brilliant.

 LOUIS: Krishnan's brilliant. He tweeted one time, 'I just made too many pancakes.' He's got a life. He does stuff when he's not on the news. And I love Maggie Smith. I don't know what it is.

 ANDREW: Ever since you were a little boy you used to like Maggie Smith. She's in *Clash of the Titans*.

 LOUIS: Yeah, she was the goddess Hera.

SID: I like Nicholas Parsons. Although he doesn't come on television any more. I think he's a real gentleman. Also John Humphrys, the *Mastermind* guy. And it's not that they're boring; they're still funny. They can be comical. And they're very clever, intelligent people. And they're not big-headed about it either. As opposed to Paxman. It's a standard, isn't it? That's how normal human beings should behave really.

LEON & JUNE, LIVERPOOL

JUNE: Tim Henman is a genuinely nice person. He was a superb player and he never made excuses. It was always, 'I didn't play as well as my opponent today.' And he had a lot of pressure. I think maybe if he hadn't had quite as much pressure, he could have won.

LEON: That's right. I always say, if I'd been the umpire when McEnroe was in his heyday, he'd have got a punch in the face.

JUNE: Although you warmed to him when he came to Calderstones because he wore an Everton shirt.

LEON: He had a number ten on his back.

REV. KATE & GRAHAM, NOTTINGHAMSHIRE

GRAHAM: Kevin McCloud.

KATE: Simon Pegg.

GRAHAM: You went to Spondon Asda to get his autograph.

KATE: I found him. I found Simon Pegg. He gave me a Jaffa Cake. I was very happy. I don't like Jaffa Cakes, but I ate it anyway because I wouldn't want to upset him. I love Simon Pegg. Like, almost in a wrong way.

GRAHAM: There are other people you admire. Like Clare Balding.

KATE: And I love Olivia Colman. She's just absolutely marvellous. Wonderful. And Jessica Hynes. I think she's great. And Kirsty Wark's fab. I like all women, don't I? I wonder what that says about me? Probably that I'm a bit of a feminist, which is probably right.

GRAHAM: Simon Pegg's not a woman.

KATE: No, but he's very much in touch with his feminine side.

Bill & Josef
Cambridge

Bill & Josef

CAMBRIDGE

———

Bill, 67, and Josef, 69, have been friends for
seventeen years. Bill, a journalist, is a former
British Chess Champion who has represented
the country in many international tournaments
and won several times. Josef, an accountant,
is the current World Cluedo Champion and
Scottish Monopoly Champion.

———

HOW DID YOU MEET?

BILL: Josef and I met on a charity walk, visiting all of the places on the Monopoly board. So it was a walk round London, but you had to go as fast as you could through all the sites, in any order you liked, but only using public transport. Of course, the army teams did best. Basically running.

BILL:

Josef and I met on a charity walk, visiting all of the places on the Monopoly board.

HOW DID YOU GET ON GOGGLEBOX?

JOSEF: They'd asked me, and they wanted two people. But there's no way my wife is going to appear on television. So I thought, 'Who do I know who's stupid enough to do this programme?' So I phoned up Bill.

BILL: No, you didn't. It was a complete accident. We just happened to bump into each other. You just said, 'Would you be interested in appearing in a television programme with me?' And I said, 'Is it stupid?' And he said, 'Yeah.' So I said, 'Fine – let's do it.'

JOSEF: I thought it'd be a one-off programme. Turns out I was wrong.

BILL: When the *Gogglebox* team rang me to say they wanted us, they said, 'Just one thing – that painting behind you ...' I was sure they were going to say it had to be covered, or would have to come down. And they said, 'Could we have the name of the artist?' To ask permission to show it. It was painted by Rebecca Ivatts, who was a neighbour of mine. She lived next door and I knew she was only here temporarily. I was feeding her occasionally – giving her biscuits – and eventually I saw her paintings and that was the one that I really liked. So I said, don't leave Cambridge without selling it to me. So when she left, I bought it.

There was a really funny moment – she and her parents were in Cambridge, after she'd left, and her father was sitting here peering at the painting, and saying it had always been his favourite of hers, and he was glad it had found a good home. And he was just looking at the hands above and he said, 'Er ... Rebecca ... those are your hands, aren't they?' And she said, 'Yes, Daddy.' And this look came over his face when he realised the rest of it was her as well ...

> **JOSEF:**
> Now we are known as either 'the intelligent couple' or the 'couple with the boobs painting'.

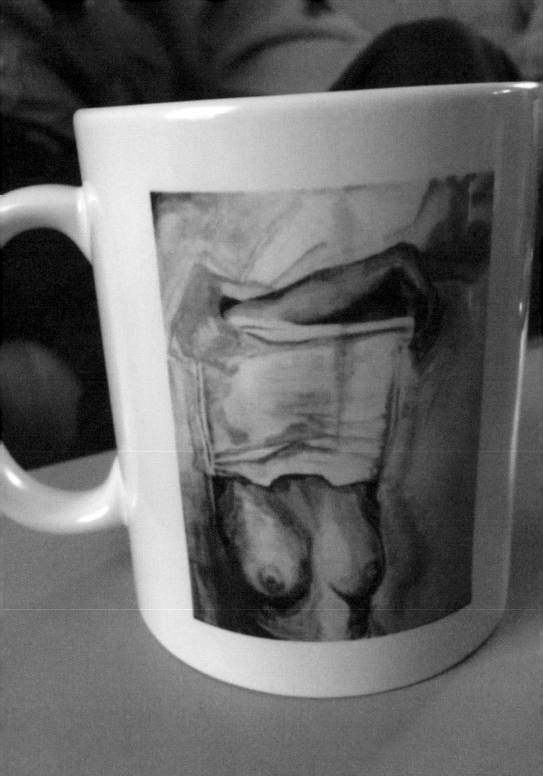

Bill as a finalist on BBC 2's
The Master Game chess
tournament, 14 February 1977

HAD YOU BEEN ON TV BEFORE?

BILL: Yes. I first appeared as a commentator on programmes we did on the Fischer–Spassky world championship match in 1972, then I won the first two *Master Game* series, on which I went on to become a commentator. (By far the world's best TV chess programmes of all time, incidentally.) *Play Chess*, which I presented, was a spin-off from that. We got audiences of two million.

BILL:

I won the first two Master Game series… (By far the world's best TV chess programmes of all time, incidentally.)

I was British Champion before we had any good players. The generation after mine overtook my generation so quickly and comprehensively that there came a moment when I either had to work very hard to avoid falling even further behind them, or just take it all a bit less seriously and earn a living by writing about them instead.

I also played *Mastermind* with Derren Brown on one of his programmes when he'd asked for some chess players to pit his wits against. I was very happy to let him get his tricks right, because I knew they wouldn't use my bits if he got them wrong. I had dinner with him around that time, incidentally, and we agreed to meet in a restaurant in Covent Garden. I got there early and was shown to the table where I sat for about half an hour waiting for him. Then I wandered off to see if he was waiting somewhere else, and found him sitting at the bar wondering where I'd got to. My opinion of his mind-reading skills dropped considerably (though he's a very interesting person to have dinner with).

JOSEF: I've done *Fifteen to One* and *Countdown*. GMTV have broadcast live from my cottage, showing my collection of board games. And *Collector's Lot* also featured it. I have approximately 180 editions of Monopoly and about 110 Scrabble – different languages and special editions…

BILL: There are seventeen As in Malaysian Scrabble, you know. That's the highest number of any letter in any edition.

Josef as Colonel Mustard,
winner of the World Cluedo
Championship, 1993

THE OSTRICH IN ANCIENT AND
MODERN TIMES

BILL: I used to know Russell Ash. I commissioned him to write five columns in place of me, to fill one of my spots. And he wrote the five pieces on books with bizarre titles, getting more and more bizarre, until the last one was about someone at the Field Museum of Anthropology in Chicago, a guy called Berthold Laufer, who wrote a series of pamphlets with absolutely ridiculous titles. And Russell wrote, 'There is one title which establishes this man as absolutely the most bizarre book writer of all time, which is *Ostrich Egg-shell Cups of Mesopotamia and the Ostrich in Ancient and Modern Times.*' When I got the manuscript of his column, I just happened to have a copy of that book in my bag, so I photocopied the title page and faxed it to him. And he rang me up and said, 'I might have known. If anyone would have a copy of that, it would be you.'

> **BILL:**
> I just happened to have a copy of that book in my bag.

FIELD MUSEUM OF NATURAL HISTORY
DEPARTMENT OF ANTHROPOLOGY
CHICAGO, 1926

LEAFLET   NUMBER 23

Ostrich Egg-shell Cups of Mesopotamia
and the Ostrich in Ancient and
Modern Times

CONTENTS

WHAT DO YOU THINK
OF YOURSELVES ON SCREEN?

BILL: I think, 'That's me.' I don't feel I'm doing anything special or unusual or different for the programme. I reviewed a book for the *Independent* years ago about eccentrics, written by a psychologist. And he made this stupid mistake – and the whole book was completely flawed – because he'd asked for people who considered themselves eccentric, which eccentrics don't.

JOSEF: Eccentrics are normal.

BILL: They just consider everybody else is eccentric.

JOSEF: Norman Wisdom presented me with an award for being one of the UK's top ten eccentrics.

BILL: Norman Wisdom is the only person to have been given the Freedom of Tirana, Albania, without also having won a Nobel Prize.

JOSEF: Yeah. They're massive fans. Anyway, I was given an award for being eccentric because of my collection of board games, and the fact that I dress up as Colonel Mustard when I'm playing Cluedo, and I've got a big Monopoly suit I've had made especially, and I've played Rummikub in the bath and other weird things. For example, Radio Luxembourg once had a competition and the prize was to be a princess for four days. So I entered. And I won. And they said, 'But it's a girls' competition.' And I said, 'It doesn't say in the rules it's a girls' competition.' They said, 'No, it doesn't. Well, OK, so you won. You're a princess for four days.' The idea was, I was to be given a tiara and a mannequin parade, but they didn't think I'd be interested in that, so instead I was given a stopwatch and taken to a strip club.

BILL: Danny Simon's recipe for a successful sitcom was basically: define your characters well, and leave them to do the writing for you. The characters should be human archetypes but taken one step further. They should have all human weaknesses but a little bit further than the viewer's. And I think that's the real key to the success of *Gogglebox*: that we're all outrageous, absurd characters in a way that everybody is outrageous and absurd, but taken one step further.

BEING RECOGNISED

BILL: In the last week I've been identified by several people, which I find very surprising because I've had an extreme haircut. And so even in the wrong place, wearing glasses, disguised with a haircut, people still point me out.

JOSEF: I've just come back from Alaska...

BILL: The only American state you can type on one row of a keyboard...

JOSEF: He's full of rubbish like this. Anyway, the steward on the plane said, 'Oh, you're on *Gogglebox*, aren't you?' And I said yes. And one of his mates said, 'What's *Gogglebox*?' And he said, 'Oh, you've got to watch it. It's my wife's favourite programme.'

BILL: Peru is the only country you can type on one row of a keyboard. It's a different row, of course.

JOSEF: We went to a Christmas fair in Southampton, near where I live, and this woman came charging up to me and said, 'I'm arguing with my friends: are you on *Gogglebox*?' I said yes. 'But it says Cambridge on the show.' I said, I travel to Cambridge every week to do the filming. 'More fool you,' she said, and walked off.

BILL: A few years ago, Mark Borkowski – he's a PR man – was writing a book called *The Fame Formula*. I've known him for years, and he knows about my mathematical upbringing, and he said he'd been thinking about the idea that everyone's famous for fifteen minutes. And he thought that, even if that was true when Warhol said it, he didn't think it was true any more. And he asked me if I could find out how long people are famous for now.

So I did an analysis for him. I took people like the winners of *Britain's Got Talent*, who'd shot to fame from nothing, or people who'd been sort of travelling along at a fair level and then won an Oscar – and I ended up with the discovery that you are not famous for fifteen minutes, you're famous for fifteen months. And after that, you get back to the level of fame you were at before.

BILL:
I'm very surprised at being recognised.

Bill's mug collection

WOULD YOU NORMALLY WATCH TV TOGETHER?

JOSEF: Oh no. If he came down to see me, I doubt if we'd watch television.

BILL: I rarely watch television. The only programmes I watch are *Saturday Kitchen* and *The Big Bang Theory*.

JOSEF: I know why you watch *The Big Bang Theory*. Who's the most pedantic on that programme?

BILL: What, Sheldon? I can identify with Sheldon.

JOSEF: You are Sheldon. You are the most pedantic pedant I know.

BILL: Thank you. Nicest thing you've ever said about me.

JOSEF: I watch *Mastermind*, *University Challenge*, *Have I Got News for You* and I might put *Countryfile* on in the background while I'm doing something else. Doing *Gogglebox* has educated us in one sense, because we've watched programmes we wouldn't normally have watched, and we have found them interesting. (Or we've thought, now I know why I don't watch it, because it's such a load of dross.)

BILL: Some things are so bad that they are enjoyable.

JOSEF: Yes. For instance, who in their right mind is going to have sex in a box and then discuss it? I couldn't believe that anybody would make that kind of programme.

BILL:
I divide everything into a good idea well executed, a good idea badly executed, a bad idea well executed or a bad idea badly executed. And Sex Box was definitely the last of them.

WHAT DO YOU DISAGREE ON?

JOSEF: Well, we do have arguments. Like, we'll be watching, for example, *Britain's Got Talent*, and he'll say 'What a rubbish programme,' and I'll say, well, *you* think it's terrible, but millions don't agree with you.

BILL: So they're wrong.

JOSEF: The fact that you don't like a particular programme and millions do means it doesn't appeal to you. It doesn't mean the programme's wrong, it's just that your tastes are different.

BILL: I don't mind what other people watch. I just said it was rubblish. It is rubbish.

JOSEF: You won't be happy until people are only watching things like *Newsnight*.

BILL: A week or two ago we watched *Alan Carr: Chatty Man*. I'd never watched that before. But I took an instant dislike to Alan Carr. I don't know why.

JOSEF: Because he's chatty.

BILL: There's this lovely quote of someone who asked, 'Why is it that people take an instant dislike to me?' and the person he was talking to said, 'Because it saves time.'

JOSEF: People seem to think I like Graham Norton. I don't know why. Certain things on his show have been interesting, but I have never once said I like Graham Norton.

GARY BARLOW

STEPH & DOM, SANDWICH

 DOM: Squeaky clean. Not quite so with his tax bill.

 STEPH: I've got a bit of a crush on him. I know everyone thinks he's very dull. But he did that lovely thing for that lady when he turned up at her wedding and came out through the catering tent and started singing. Oh, it was lovely. That made me cry. I think, actually, he's a very decent human being and a nice bloke. He's been up; he's been down; he's been up; he's been down. I don't know, there's something cute about his face. Don't know quite what it is.

SANDY & SANDRA, BRIXTON

 SANDRA: When we saw Gary Barlow on TV the other night in that programme with James Corden, we thought, 'Oh right,' and we sussed him out. And we were feeling sorry for him and whatever, and, hey, two days later I say, 'Sandy! Big scandal! And he's got to give back the OBE!' Fucking dickhead.

 SANDY: He went through a lot though. I mean, he's not the only one that went through obesity or whatever when he was younger. And a lot of people didn't know that storyline, so it was a good way to show that side of him. But he does talk a bit slow. He does, doesn't he? He takes hours.

THE MOFFATS, COUNTY DURHAM

 BETTY: He reminds me of Elton John but I do like him. But it's just… It's his voice, isn't it? It's really…

 SCARLETT: …boring.

 MARK: Boring.

LEON & JUNE, LIVERPOOL

 LEON: Gary Barlow's as thick as the wall.

SCARLETT:
I think he looks like a Primark version of Robbie Williams, but Mam really likes him.

JOSÉ MOURINHO

STEPHEN & CHRIS, BRIGHTON

 CHRIS: So he's the manager of the guy that's just got the three goals? You'd have thought he'd be a bit happier than that, wouldn't you?

 STEPHEN: He's French. They ain't happy, are they?

STEPHEN FRY

LINDA, PETE & GEORGE, CLACTON-ON-SEA

 PETE: Me and George, we watch the Discovery Channel, and people like Stephen Fry. We love him. He's funny, brilliant, genius. He knows stuff. And when I saw that one about the gays, I actually had tears in my eyes when I saw that part, in Iran, when they hanged them. It doesn't matter what you are, does it, for Christ's sake?

 GEORGE: If there is anyone that I'd like to meet off the TV on a serious note, number one would be David Attenborough, and number two would be Stephen Fry. I don't know why. I probably wouldn't even know what he was saying to me. But I just think he's brilliant.

THE BECKHAMS

STEPHEN & CHRIS, BRIGHTON

 STEPHEN: Victoria, bless her, she's got really piss-fine hair, hasn't she? That's why it only ever looks good in a bob.

 CHRIS: David's always had good hair. Apart from the curtains that he started out with.

REV. KATE & GRAHAM, NOTTINGHAMSHIRE

 KATE: David Beckham's very cute. I'm not after a conversation with him. He can stick to the vowel sounds as far as I'm concerned.

THE MOFFATTS, COUNTY DURHAM

 BETTY: They're perfect. There's nothing else to say, they're just perfect.

JOSÉ:
I'm from Portugal...

STEPHEN:
Golden balls? They'd be black and blue, time I'd finished with them.

STEPH:

I'd quite like to be Victoria's fat friend. Every thin bird needs a fatfriend, and I'd like to be hers. We'd go out on the piss together. And we'd go shopping for chubby clothes.

STEPHEN & CHRIS, BRIGHTON

 STEPHEN: Jeremy Clarkson.

 CHRIS: Jeremy Clarkson.

 STEPHEN: That doctor as well. What's his name?

 CHRIS: Dr Christian...

 STEPHEN: Yeah, the one that looks like Action Man.

THE MICHAELS, BRIGHTON

 CAROLYNE: Top of my hit list is Carol Vorderman. She's just so up herself. Thinks she's God's gift.

 LOUIS: She thinks she knows all the consonants and all the vowels.

 ANDREW: My list is just Simon Cowell and Russell Brand. Telling people not to vote, when people put down their lives for the advancement of democracy. And not offering us any alternatives! That's what pseudo people actually do. I think it's immoral.

 CAROLYNE: And you don't like Simon Cowell because he exploits people.

 ANDREW: No, I just don't like his teeth. They're too white and they dazzle me.

STEPH & DOM, SANDWICH

 STEPH: Keith Lemon. He's a knob.

 DOM: John Sessions. Absolute twat. Needs a good punch.

STEPH: I think John Cleese is a bit of a prat as well. Putting that out there.

BILL & JOSEF, CAMBRIDGE

 BILL: Alan Carr. He's the very opposite of a deadpan comic. He's not funny and he's not deadpan. Everything about him is just so offputting. My opinion of Graham Norton went up a notch when I discovered Alan Carr.

THE TAPPERS, NORTH LONDON

 JOSH: Kirstie Allsopp. She's stuck up. She thinks she's above everyone else.

 JONATHAN: She got very upset when *Gogglebox* slated her crafts programme.

 NIKKI: It was very painful. It was so dull.

SANDY & SANDRA, BRIXTON

 SANDRA: I love everyone on TV. I love them all. Between me and her, and I can vouch for her and vouch for myself: we're lovers. Not like me and her are lovers, like, us two together. But we don't hate anyone. We love everybody.

 SANDY: Yeah, love, not hate.

LINDA, PETE & GEORGE, CLACTON-ON-SEA

 GEORGE: Me. Simple. Game over. Me. Give me the opportunity, I will be the biggest prat on TV.

BAASIT:

I don't like Jonathan Ross. He's another one who should act his age. Some of the stuff that he says is borderline embarrassing for a man of his age.

SANDY & SANDRA, BRIXTON

 SANDRA: Well, I've got a crush on Alan Carr.

 SANDY: Tom Jones you love.

 SANDRA: I'd throw my knickers at Tom Jones. He'd get the bra as well, mate. Trust me.

THE MOFFATTS, COUNTY DURHAM

 SCARLETT: I like loads. Russell Howard. George Lamb.

 MARK: You used to fancy Bart Simpson at one point.

 BETTY: And Noddy.

 SCARLETT: Aye, but I was little, Mam!

 MARK: Betty used to like Troy Tempest. Out of *Thunderbirds*.

 BETTY: No! No! I just said that if you had to go out with a puppet, then Troy Tempest was the best-looking one.

 MARK: Where would you take him? Would you go down the pub?

 BETTY: No, probably not.

 SCARLETT: Settle for a champagne bar.

 BETTY: Just for a meal and then just out for drinks somewhere, I think.

 SCARLETT: What would he eat, like?

 BETTY: I don't think he'd be fussy, to be fair. Not got a digestive system.

MARK: Courteney Cox. I like her.

BETTY: Oh! Or Robert De Niro.

 SCARLETT: He's more film, isn't he?

 BETTY: OK. Troy Tempest will do. I'd have to carry him.

THE MICHAELS, BRIGHTON

 CAROLYNE: I've got a crush on Russell Brand, but you can't say that. Oh, Alan Rickman! I'm completely in love with Alan Rickman.

 LOUIS: Alan Rickman is a *Gogglebox* watcher and he said that I was a bright and clever boy.

 ANDREW: There is someone I like. Who is it I like?

 CAROLYNE: Nigella Lawson.

 ANDREW: Oh my God, I love Nigella Lawson.

 CAROLYNE: For fuck's sake.

 LOUIS: You like Mary Berry, don't you, Dad?

 ANDREW: I don't!

 LOUIS: I'm just taking the piss.

 ANDREW: I don't like any women apart from Nigella Lawson and my wife.

STEPH & DOM, SANDWICH

 DOM: Steph.

 STEPH: Yeah. Me. Me. Talk about me.

 DOM: It's always about you, darling.

JOSEF: Felicity Kendal. In *The Good Life*. That was such a good programme, you'd think they really were married. The perfect cast, in my opinion. You've got Tom and Margo next door. Jerry was the perfect henpecked husband and Margo was the perfect I'm-better-than-the-Joneses wife. And you've selfish Tom and his self-sufficiency thing, and the faithful Barbara who did what her husband wanted. And I thought to myself, you are so perfectly matched, the four of you. And Felicity herself, I thought, yeah, I've fallen in love with you. She was great.

 BILL: Monica Galetti from *Masterchef*. She is real scary. I like her passion for what she's doing. Very interesting and fascinating to me. I'd really like to meet her.

Almost always, after *Saturday Kitchen*, I go into the kitchen and cook something. It really produces a passion. It makes me want to go and play in the kitchen. A few weeks ago, Daniel Clifford (who is the two Michelin-starred chef at Midsummer House, just across the way) did a very simple thing with lamb's liver, which I immediately downloaded and cooked. And it's wonderful.

THE SIDDIQUIS, DERBY

 UMAR: I used to have a crush on Michaela Strachan. Currently though, I like the *Countdown* girl.

 BAASIT: Yeah, she's hot. Good with numbers as well. Which is always important. Dad liked Nigella Lawson. *[Makes tiger noise]*

 SID: We all have a soft spot for her.

SCARLETT:

I proper love Alan Carr. I love his teeth, they look like they're having a party.

UMAR: Well, you two do.

 SID: Don't you?

 UMAR: No.

 SID: Something wrong with you.

THE TAPPERS, NORTH LONDON

 JONATHAN: Michelle Keegan.

 JOSH: Mila Kunis.

 NIKKI: George Clooney.

 AMY: Harry Styles.

 JONATHAN: Cara from *Studio Nights*.

 NIKKI: *Studio Nights*?

 JONATHAN: On Babestation.

 AMY: She's the boobs on the wallpaper on his phone.

BETTY:
Troy Tempest. I'd have to carry him.

TV
PRESENTERS

ANT & DEC

THE TAPPERS, NORTH LONDON

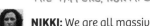

NIKKI: We are all massive fans of Ant and Dec in the Tapper household.

JOSH: Ant and Dec are the best people on TV.

AMY: Mum and Dad had a dressing-up party and they went as PJ and Duncan.

JONATHAN: We looked nothing like them.

NIKKI: You know they're huge fans of *Gogglebox*?

JOSH: When on *Saturday Night Takeaway* they did their version of *Gogglebox*, I felt so privileged.

NIKKI: They're huge fans of the show, in fact they tweeted after the BAFTAs, like 'We got a BAFTA!' So George, from Linda, Pete and George, put, 'So did we!'

JEREMY KYLE

THE WOERDENWEBERS, THE WIRRAL

RALF: For me, he is two-faced because he tells people in their faces what they doing wrong, and he cheated on his wife.

VIV: We've been to see *Jeremy Kyle*.

EVE: Jezza! He told Jay to take off his hat when we were in the audience. When he told him to take the hat off, I perked up. Because I wanted to talk to Jeremy Kyle, I went, 'I don't like this hat,' and Jeremy was like, 'Right, the lady doesn't like your hat. Take it off or I'll kick you out the studio.' I was like, 'Jeremy, I love you.'

JEREMY CLARKSON

SANDY & SANDRA, BRIXTON

 SANDY: He's a dickhead. He gets away with it because of money. There's a lot of people that watch the show, because it's a motor show with cars and all that. If it was somebody else, they would have got sacked for their behaviour. He's got away with it too many times and they still allow him to do it. Obviously it's not his looks or anything else, it's just the money, isn't it?

LEON & JUNE, LIVERPOOL

 JUNE: It's the *Top Gear* guy.

 LEON: Kenneth Clarkson, is it?

 JUNE: No, Jeremy Clarkson.

 LEON: He's a bully and a nasty man. Arrogant pig.

LINDA, PETE & GEORGE, CLACTON-ON-SEA

 PETE: I think a lot of what he says is deliberate. And they can't get rid of him, because he's too far up the tree, isn't he? I think a lot of it is shock tactics with the bloke. The actual show is brilliant, but he does seem to put his foot in it.

THE MOFFATTS, COUNTY DURHAM

 BETTY: I just think he's overrated. Fourteen million, was it, he made last year?

 SCARLETT: I Googled it. And he's got a face like a sponge. And this proper mundane voice, droning on. He's like a fun sponge.

THE TAPPERS, NORTH LONDON

 JONATHAN: I like him.

NIKKI: I think *Top Gear*'s become a really good programme.

 JOSH: Mum! You don't watch it.

STEPHEN & CHRIS, BRIGHTON

 STEPHEN: Anyone that passionate about a fucking car has got something wrong with them.

BETTY:

He always looks as if he's trying to be a trendy art teacher or something.

261

STEPH & DOM, SANDWICH

STEPH & DOM, SANDWICH

 STEPH: He's a knob. But I like him.

 DOM: I wouldn't mind putting him in charge of the country for about six months. That could be quite entertaining.

THE SIDDIQUIS, DERBY

 SID: He's a classic one for letting his mouth run away. And then once he's done that, he realises and then he's apologetic about it. I don't like the man, full stop. The whole attitude about him, his arrogance, the way he dresses.

 UMAR: It just seems like he's been suffering a very, very long midlife crisis.

LEON & JUNE, LIVERPOOL

 JUNE: That's a nice way to see Africa, isn't it? At the country's expense.

BRIAN COX

THE MICHAELS, BRIGHTON

 CAROLYNE: Brian Cox? He makes me want to go to sleep.

STEPHEN:
It's like he's on f****ing drugs, ain't he? 'Oh, yeah! The stars!'

BRUCE FORSYTH

REV. KATE & GRAHAM, NOTTINGHAMSHIRE

GRAHAM: He needs to go home now.

LEON & JUNE, LIVERPOOL

JUNE: We go back to *Sunday Night at the London Palladium* with Bruce Forsyth. He's stood the test of time, hasn't he? OK, he's fluffed his lines, but is that the end of the world? It shows he's human.

SANDY & SANDRA, BRIXTON

SANDY: I met him when I was very young. I used to sing, when I was three, 'til I was five years of age. In the Tower, in Blackpool. And I met Bruce Forsyth, and Larry Grayson and a few others. I used to sing 'My Old Man's A Dustman'.

JEREMY PAXMAN

STEPH & DOM, SANDWICH

DOM: He's ageing, isn't he? He's starting to look like a bloodhound.

STEPH: I was about to say he looks like his face is melting. Like a candle.

SIMON COWELL

THE TAPPERS, NORTH LONDON

NIKKI: Genius.

JONATHAN: Pain in the arse.

THE MOFFATTS, COUNTY DURHAM

 BETTY: I think he'd be a brilliant prime minister. I don't know what the hell he'd do.

 MARK: He'd take the shite away.

STEPH & DOM, SANDWICH

 STEPH: Short.

 DOM: Sharp.

 STEPH: Machiavellian.

 DOM: Ballsy.

 STEPH: Bad skin.

SCARLETT:

He has boobs and high-waisted trousers, and yet everybody fancies him. He must be doing something right. He's a proper DILF.

SANDY & SANDRA, BRIXTON

 SANDRA: Guess what I dreamt about? I told them, when I woke up, I said no word of a lie at all. Simon Cowell. I dream a lot about stars. Simon Cowell, I like him, I like him. Before even this dream, I like him. I like the way he's stern, I like the way his trousers are up there.

 SANDY: And he'll never get rid of Sinitta.

STEPHEN & CHRIS, BRIGHTON

 STEPHEN: If I was there, I'd chuck a cup of piss over him.

THE WOERDENWEBERS, THE WIRRAL

 RALF: We have someone like him in Germany. His name is Dieter Bohlen in Germany, the man who is Simon Cowell in England. If I show you the jury in Germany and I put them in different places and I ask you who is the Simon Cowell, and you'll say straightaway, 'He!' And you never saw him in his life.

EVE: I thought he would have been a bit nicer since he's had a kid now.

RALF: But if I, as a musician, go on the stage, I couldn't take it from him. It doesn't matter, if he's saying I'm shit, then I'm shit. That's what I have to take. But I would say to him, 'Can you sing?' I would say to him, 'Have you ever wrote your own song? I have. I have made six CDs already, you know? So I will take it, yeah, but don't be so nasty. Because you see from the business side and not from the musical side.'

LEON & JUNE, LIVERPOOL

 LEON: Sneering prat.

 JUNE: I've been trying to find out what his talent is. All that money and, well…how did he get it? What is his talent? What has he done? And why has he got a name like Simon Callow? Because I love Simon Callow.

The Tappers
North London

The Tappers

NORTH LONDON

———

The Tappers are Jonathan, 47, an executive driver,
and Nikki, 41, a nursery teacher.
Their two children are Josh, 17, and Amy, 14, who
is the youngest contributor on *Gogglebox*.
They live in North London.

———

HOW DID YOU MEET?

NIKKI: We met on holiday. But it wasn't really a holiday romance.

JONATHAN: We met in Eilat. In Israel.

JOSH: He proposed to her two months after they met.

AMY: In a car. And his mum called halfway through asking if he'd done it yet.

NIKKI: I should have known, when your mother rang in the middle of you proposing to me, what my life was going to be like.

JONATHAN: You don't even speak to my mother.

NIKKI: I do.

JONATHAN: When?

NIKKI: Occasionally.

NIKKI:
We met on holiday. But it wasn't really a holiday romance.

AMY: Anyway, she said yes. So obviously she was desperate.

NIKKI: No, I definitely wasn't desperate. But your father was. Eighteen years. It's our anniversary next week. Eighteen years.

JONATHAN: I'm not celebrating now. That I can assure you.

AMY: Dad, if you take mum for dinner, why can't me and Josh come with you?

JONATHAN: Because it's our anniversary, not yours.

JOSH: Yeah, but I want dinner.

AMY: Father, can I get takeaway?

NIKKI: We went on honeymoon to San Francisco, Maui and Las Vegas. And we had one of the best holidays apart from I cried the whole way there.

JONATHAN: The whole plane journey.

NIKKI: How old was I? Twenty-three? I had lived at home, never moved out. I'd been travelling, but I'd never actually left home. And then I moved out the day we got married. And I was just, like, 'Whoah!' We got married yesterday and we got on a plane the following morning, and I just think I found the whole thing overwhelming.

269

HOW DID YOU GET ON GOGGLEBOX?

NIKKI: I did a programme on Channel 4 called *Jewish Mum of the Year*, which I have to tell you was *absolutely horrendous*. People nominated people to do it and you went through all these workshops. My mum put me forward.

JONATHAN: What she was saying is that she's *not* Jewish Mother of the Year, but her daughter is.

NIKKI: The final ten were on telly, and I was in the final twelve, so I never got on TV. But one of the researchers had come to the house and interviewed the kids, and she rang me completely out the blue six months later, trying to find households to do this new programme, *Gogglebox*. I thought it would be brilliant.

JONATHAN: If she'd gone all the way on the *Jewish Mum* show, we would never have done this, though.

NIKKI: Everything they said the programme wasn't going to be, it was. And believe me, you were not portrayed in the way you wanted to be portrayed.

JONATHAN: It was car-crash comedy.

NIKKI: I told *Gogglebox* exactly what I thought of the experience doing the *Jewish Mum* programme, and they said this show was going to be nothing like that.

JONATHAN: From Day One, I said I wouldn't do this show if it's going be anything like *Come Dine with Me*, where I find it funny but I wouldn't want to be on the other end of it.

JOSH: That's the good thing about *Gogglebox*. They don't want to take the piss out of us. They want us to entertain everyone.

Josh (7) and Amy (4), 2004

HAD YOU BEEN ON TV BEFORE?

JONATHAN: I once nearly got kicked off *Top of the Pops*. It was nothing major. Years ago. Gary Davies was the DJ and I was in the audience. And he was introducing the next act: it was after Murray Head doing 'One Night In Bangkok', and going into Paul McCartney's 'Frog Chorus'. I was standing next to him, and I got my hand over his head, and went and did the rabbit ears. And then, afterwards, the producer came up and had a go at me, and said they'd have to reshoot the whole thing again. But they didn't. It was on. I've got it on video.

JOSH: Sorry, what? What's this?

NIKKI: I was on *Top of the Pops*, too, one time, dancing in the background to Five Star. And I was on *Grange Hill* as well.

AMY: Why do you not tell us *anything*?

NIKKI: I went to a big school in Elstree. When I was eleven or twelve, they asked our school for extras. And it was for the first day of term at *Grange Hill* and it was a massive episode, all in the hall. We met all of them because we spent the whole day with them. Ziggy was in it at the time.

JONATHAN: What was the little fat one they used to take the mickey out of?

NIKKI: Roland.

JONATHAN: Roland is the Augustus Gloop of *Grange Hill*. She calls me Augustus Gloop. So you ended up marrying your Roland.

NIKKI: Ziggy was in it, Banksy was in it. There was Ant. And that Jewish boy.

JONATHAN: Dec?

NIKKI: It was brilliant. I think Ziggy had been really naughty and taken a spider into the assembly and it escaped from his pocket.

JONATHAN: I only remember Tucker Jenkins and Roland.

JOSH: I have *no* idea what you're talking about.

> **NIKKI:**
> I was in Grange Hill as well.

WHAT DO YOU THINK
OF YOURSELVES ON SCREEN?

JOSH: You just start laughing.

NIKKI: It's like a video of yourself. A home video.

AMY: We don't see it in the way that fans would, or other people. And neither do my friends. So my friends don't understand how big it actually is. They just watch it and they see me, and they're, like, 'It was really funny.' And then they're out with me and I get stopped for a picture or something and then they'll be like, 'Oh my God! This is actually quite a big programme.'

JONATHAN: Every year, for this festival called Purim, the school makes a pro video. And this year, they wanted to give us the video, and film us watching it. And then they edited us watching the Purim video into the actual thing. And it got played at school.

AMY: Everyone just screamed.

Jonathan and Nikki on their wedding day,
27 May 1996

BEING RECOGNISED

JOSH: Me and Amy went out to the cinema in Borehamwood, by Elstree Studios, with Grandma and Papa. And we had just left the cinema when I saw that someone recognised us.

AMY: I see this figure coming up to me from the right, and there's this young, really pretty woman, just standing there on the phone. And this man comes up to me and says, 'Excuse me, you're the kid from *Gogglebox*, aren't you?'

JOSH: And then I walked round and I stopped and I went, 'You're Rufus Hound!'

AMY: And my Papa, he's obsessed with *Strictly Come Dancing*. So he goes, 'Oh my God, that's Flavia'. He was so excited, because he couldn't believe that they stopped his grandchildren.

JOSH: Us. They stopped us. And they asked *us* for a picture.

AMY: At this point, my papa grabs Flavia and goes, 'Come on, let's have a photo.' And he's got it up on his desk at work. His girlfriend and his wife.

NIKKI: We were at this party and the next thing you know this photo is uploaded onto Twitter. Of Rufus Hound with our kids. And it's so random. He's written, 'Just guess who I bumped into? The *Gogglebox* kids.' And we're at this party, completely wetting ourselves laughing. So Jonathan sent him a message to say, 'Hope they're behaving themselves.'

JOSH: And Rufus Hound sends a message back, going, 'No, they're round the back of Gala bingo, sniffing glue with their gran and granddad.'

AMY: Dad just put, 'A standard Sunday night,' in return. Something like that.

> **AMY:**
> And this man comes up to me and says, 'Excuse me, you're the kid from Gogglebox, aren't you?'

> **JOSH:**
> And then I walked round and I stopped and I went, 'You're Rufus Hound!'

277

WOULD YOU NORMALLY
WATCH TV TOGETHER?

JOSH: Before *Gogglebox*, we didn't much sit down, just the four of us.

AMY: Dad's normally working. Mum's in the kitchen. Or on the phone. But we'd watch *X Factor* or *Britain's Got Talent*.

JONATHAN: One of the big shows.

NIKKI: Even if everyone goes out on a Saturday night, we'll record family shows and then, on Sunday, we'll all sit down and watch it. We used to sit and watch TV a lot more all together when the kids were younger.

AMY: But when it comes to programmes, we enjoy different things now. Like I enjoy trash like *Geordie Shore* or *TOWIE*.

JOSH: She likes all the rubbish. Me and Dad, we like watching American action programmes like *Hawaii Five-0*.

JONATHAN: It's not really like the original. McGarrett is a totally different character. He's an ex-Navy SEAL. It's very well done.

AMY: I watch *Gossip Girl* on Netflix. I'm obsessed with it. I've got nearly up to the end, and it's six series. Each one is twenty-five episodes and I've watched them for, like, two months. Dad watches *Gossip Girl* – sometimes. He pretends he doesn't like it but he secretly does.

JONATHAN: I do not. I do not.

AMY: When he sits down to watch it with me he loves it.

JONATHAN: It's called not having a choice.

AMY: Before I started watching *Gossip Girl*, I watched the last episode.

JOSH: Ruined the whole storyline.

AMY: Sometimes I go to the end of something, just to see the ending and then I'll rewind back and enjoy all the pieces coming together. I'm reading a book at the moment on my phone, which is some fan fiction of One Direction. But it updates every week, so I can't go to the end of the book.

> **AMY:**
> Dad watches Gossip Girl – sometimes. He pretends that he doesn't like it but he secretly does.

WHAT'S YOUR FAVOURITE
THING TO WATCH?

JONATHAN: She only really watches the phone.

JOSH: She's like, 'I'm going to sit down, I'm going to sit down and watch TV...' And then she sits down, and the phone rings.

NIKKI: I'm a bit of a chatterer on the phone.

JOSH: She's on it for about a couple of hours and then the phone rings again. And she never ends up watching TV.

And then she complains she didn't have time to relax.

JONATHAN: I don't think she's ever seen a whole programme.

NIKKI: I used to watch *Casualty* and *Holby City*. And then the best thing on TV happened: *Brothers & Sisters*. And every week it was on, I'd not only end up crying, I'd end up hyperventilating. In my bed, every week, hyperventilating, thinking, 'Why have I put myself through this?' It was the best thing on telly.

WHAT DOES TV
MEAN TO YOU?

JOSH: I don't know what life would be like without a TV, honestly.

NIKKI: He's a proper telly addict. For me it's family time. Having fun together.

JONATHAN: It's entertainment, but I use it for information as well...

NIKKI: You use it for schluffing.

JONATHAN: Yeah. For schluffing.

NIKKI: Snoring. He sleeps through it.

279

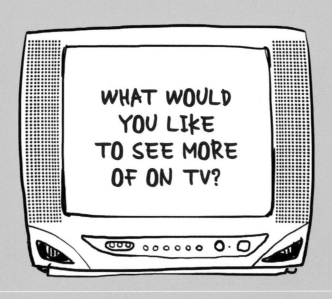

STEPHEN & CHRIS, BRIGHTON

STEPHEN: More good dramas, like *Broadchurch* and *Breaking Bad*. Things like that.

CHRIS: One of my favourite programmes was *Beautiful People*, which Olivia Colman was in. I love that sort of stuff, because it's family life but it's funny as well, so I'd like more of that sort of thing. Comedy with that touch of escapism.

STEPHEN: Anything with Julia Davis in it. I love her. *Nighty Night* was fucking brilliant. And *Human Remains*. My favourite one of them is when she's got the big glasses and she goes, 'I'm not pregnant as such, but it could happen any time. Steven's got quite a temper.' Fucking dark.

CHRIS: Oh, *The League of Gentlemen*, that's great. I think what we need a bit more of is comedy that's got more shock factor.

BILL & JOSEF, CAMBRIDGE

BILL: Useless research programmes. There's so much fun stuff done on animal behaviour. I wrote a book a few years ago called *The Things That Nobody Knows*, which is 501 questions that we don't know the answers to. It's a tour around the boundaries of human ignorance. And the very last question is: why do squirrels masturbate? And I found this piece of research by an American academic watching the masturbatory habits of Namibian squirrels. And the problem was that all the theories of masturbation would have predicted that it's the ones who are getting the least sex that were doing it most – but, in fact, with the Namibian squirrels it's the other way round.

JOSEF: He's touched on something which annoys me about *QI*. *QI* is quite often wrong. And it annoys me. One of the questions that Stephen Fry asked once was 'How many moons does the Earth have?' Well, of course, the answer's one. And the klaxons go. 'No, there are five, because these other four have been discovered.' And then, in a later series, they asked the same question again. And Alan Davies said five. And the klaxon's going, and they said, 'No: it's six. Another one's been discovered.'

This is utterly stupid. If you're going to do this pedantic sort of argument, there's either *one* moon because, as Alan says, it's called The Moon, not One Of The Moons, or the answer is nobody knows, because we have found six, but how many more small ones are there which haven't been picked up yet? If you're going to be pedantic, then be correctly pedantic.

 BILL: I once accused Stephen Fry of pinching items from my books, and he said, 'Let's just say we're both pinching from the same sources.'

REV. KATE & GRAHAM, NOTTINGHAMSHIRE

 GRAHAM: Greyhound racing.

 KATE: Zombie movies.

 GRAHAM: And more classical music.

 KATE: But with zombies. I'd like to see another series of *Blackadder*. Or would I like to see another series of *Blackadder*? You see, the thing that I really love about British TV is we know when to stop. American shows never know when to stop. I'd like to see more new stuff. More new comedy, more new subversive stuff. I want my licence fee to take risks. I don't want more of the same. Saturday night should be the night for TV, shouldn't it? And what we're getting fed is this mushy diet of baby food, of rusks soaked in water. And actually we need something that's going to stick in our throat a bit and make us feel a bit uncomfortable, but then make us laugh.

LINDA, PETE & GEORGE, CLACTON-ON-SEA

 GEORGE: There should be more stuff like *DIY SOS*. Those sorts of programmes that actually put the money back into helping someone. I know it's only one person, and there's loads of people that need help, but it would be quite nice. People will probably get bored of it, if there was loads of it. 'I'm not watching the *DIY SOS* channel again,' but if it was a possibility, I'd like to see more things like that.

LEON & JUNE, LIVERPOOL

 JUNE: I'd like to see more drama. *Last Tango in Halifax*. That was brilliant. And *Crimson Fields*. I'd like to see another slot like *Play for Today*, because there must be loads of brilliant young writers who are coming up with good new ideas.

 LEON: I like Susanna Reid's legs.

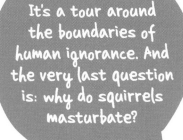

BILL:

It's a tour around the boundaries of human ignorance. And the very last question is: why do squirrels masturbate?

POLITICS

SANDY & SANDRA, BRIXTON

 SANDY: The only things I hate is all them lot that do parties. You know Labour, Liberal parties. Nothing's been changed for years. No, they piss me off when they come on, you know they do.

 SANDRA: But we don't vote or nothing like that, do we, Sandy? We don't vote. We're not a voter.

SANDY:

All of them piss me right off. Because they don't say f*** all. They say the same thing ...

REV. KATE & GRAHAM, NOTTINGHAMSHIRE

 KATE: Labour's almost impossible to recognise these days. It's such a watered-down version of itself. There's no real socialism left. It drives me mad. I've no idea who to vote for.

DAVID CAMERON

THE TAPPERS, NORTH LONDON

 JOSH: As Dad would say, he's the best of a bad bunch.

 NIKKI: Forget whether you like the Conservatives. Just as a person, the way he speaks, public speaking, how he portrays himself, how he comes across, he's the only one who actually seems like he can do it.

 JONATHAN: What tends to happen is you vote for a person, not for a party any more.

 JOSH: And that's why Labour in the next election probably won't get the votes. Because it will be Ed Miliband.

LEON: He's toadying to the Conservative right wing. He's a weak man with his woman's mouth. Oh, he's a horror.

THE MICHAELS, BRIGHTON

 ANDREW: What does a kid who's been to Eton actually know about the real world?

LINDA, PETE & GEORGE, CLACTON-ON-SEA

 GEORGE: Do you reckon he got on one knee when he proposed to Nick Clegg?

STEPHEN & CHRIS, BRIGHTON

 STEPHEN: Did he just say 'chillaxing'? Chillaxing! What a knob.

ED MILIBAND

THE MICHAELS, BRIGHTON

 LOUIS: Kermit the Frog with a red tie.

 CAROLYNE: I wouldn't vote for him because I wouldn't trust him. If he could do that to his own brother…

 ANDREW: It was open and democratic.

 LOUIS: He's a talking nose.

STEPH & DOM, SANDWICH

 DOM: Wishy-washy.

 STEPH: Knob.

 DOM: Would not command respect anywhere.

THE TAPPERS, NORTH LONDON

 NIKKI: He doesn't know how to speak.

 JONATHAN: Silly bollocks.

THE SIDDIQUIS, DERBY

 UMAR: We're warming to him.

 BAASIT: His face is too flat. If you look at his side profile, he looks a bit Lego-ish. I think he's fallen over one time too many, to be honest with you.

THE MOFFATTS, COUNTY DURHAM

 SCARLETT: Which one's that though? With the flat nose?

 MARK: He'll never be prime minister as long as I've got a hole in my bottom.

REV. KATE:
...Are you David's brother?

BAASIT:
He looks a bit Lego-ish

CHRIS: He looks like a Wallace and Gromit character. He is all *Creature Comforts*, isn't he? You know when they do their bloody party political broadcasts? He should do it as a *Creature Comforts* thing.

STEPHEN: They've all got something wrong with their mushes. Cameron's got no lips.

CHRIS: And they've all got dodgy hair.

REV. KATE & GRAHAM, NOTTINGHAMSHIRE

KATE: If I ever meet him, I'm going to go, 'Are you David's brother?'

STEPH & DOM, SANDWICH

STEPH: If you look at half his face, the top half's quite nice – bottom half's absolutely disastrous. Top half I could do. Bottom half, no fucking way.

THE WOERDENWEBERS, THE WIRRAL

RALF: 'Oh, we couldn't do this, oh, we tried so hard.' Fucking hell. They must really think we are donkeys, we're living on the tree or something with nuts under the arms. It's ridiculous.

STEPHEN & CHRIS, BRIGHTON

STEPHEN: He don't look like he could run a mile, let alone a country.

MICHAEL GOVE

LEON & JUNE, LIVERPOOL

LEON: I would shoot him if I ever saw him.

BORIS JOHNSON

THE WOERDENWEBERS, THE WIRRAL

 EVE: He's an amazing nutter.

THE SIDDIQUIS, DERBY

 BAASIT: He's just a piss-take waiting to happen.

THE MICHAELS, BRIGHTON

 ANDREW: Aren't they ghastly, these posh kids? They really turn my stomach.

 CAROLYNE: He's a twat, he's a toff, he's a fool and he's a buffoon, and it's obviously a fake…but I still like him.

STEPHEN & CHRIS, BRIGHTON

 STEPHEN: I love him.

 CHRIS: He's an idiot. Well, he *comes across* as an idiot, but I think he's quite conniving.

 STEPHEN: His family all look like each other. Have you seen his mum?

 CHRIS: She's been trimming her own fringe.

 STEPHEN: She's got teeth like a racehorse. And they've all got them thick cankles, ain't they? I reckon underneath it all he's a conniving little bastard and he's got his eyes set on that job. Smarmy pillock.

REV. KATE & GRAHAM, NOTTINGHAMSHIRE

 GRAHAM: Loveable rogue.

> **AMY:**
> I love Boris…I think it's because he reminds us of our deputy head.

KATE: Cock end.

THE SIDDIQUIS, DERBY

 UMAR: Big, pale and powerful.

 BAASIT: He's a bit like Igor's stunt double in some sort of horror film.

 SID: Or a badly dressed Tarzan.

THE MICHAELS, BRIGHTON

 CAROLYNE: Love him. He's a guilty pleasure. Like chocolate. You love it but you know you shouldn't be eating it. And it's the same with him: you love him, but you know you shouldn't. But he's just so likeable. I know it's an act, but it's clever of him because it means that people don't take him seriously.

LEON & JUNE, LIVERPOOL

 LEON: A rich buffoon. Can't stand the man.

 JUNE: He'll do anything for publicity.

STEPH & DOM, SANDWICH

 STEPH: Love him.

 DOM: Fabulous. He'd make a great PM. There are the odd occasions when I think there's so much waffle that even he doesn't know what he's saying.

THE WOERDENWEBERS, THE WIRRAL

 VIV: Oh, he's a nelly.

 RALF: I love him.

 EVE: Boris for prime minister! I want to go on a night out with him. It'd be like *The Hangover*.

VIV: He's bonkers. He's absolutely bonkers.

 EVE: Yeah, but, Mum all the best people are. How do you think I survived high school?

PETE:

That Farage drives me nuts. He's like a pantomime dame.

NIGEL FARAGE

STEPHEN & CHRIS, BRIGHTON

STEPHEN: One foot in the grave and the other one on a bar of soap.

REV. KATE & GRAHAM, NOTTINGHAMSHIRE

KATE: It's important to have somebody who is the voice of dissent, somebody who is going to hold a mirror up to it all and force people to ask questions. It's just the person that does that should be balanced and vaguely sane. He's like a naughty toddler having a tantrum in a supermarket. Stop playing to him and giving him attention, just walk away. If you just ignore him, he might stop it. Anyway, I reckon he's got a suit that he unzips and he's actually a gay woman inside with one leg.

THE MICHAELS, BRIGHTON

CAROLYNE: I love him.

LOUIS: Oh, please. Don't!

CAROLYNE: I think we feel disenfranchised and don't believe anything that any of the other politicians have told us. I don't believe that they understand what it's like to be a normal person living in today's society. I don't think they have got their finger on the pulse. And I just feel when I listen to what Nigel Farage says, it chimes.

LINDA, PETE & GEORGE, CLACTON-ON-SEA

PETE: That Farage drives me nuts. He's like a pantomime dame. 'Watch out! He's behind you!' I can't take him serious. You know what I'm saying? He's obviously far more intelligent than I am, but he just reminds me of a berk.

STEPH & DOM, SANDWICH

DOM: I've found what he's doing very interesting; refreshing, in that his approach is: 'Well, let's get on with this, do it now. What are we waiting for?

Why do we have to put it off fifteen years?' I'm not suggesting for a minute I would vote for him. I've not actually read his manifesto – in fact, I've never read anybody's manifesto. But people vote based on what they see on the telly and what they read in the paper. People are voting for people; they're not voting for policies or manifestos, they're voting…because they like him.

 STEPH: Toad of Toad Hall.

STEPHEN & CHRIS, BRIGHTON

 CHRIS: Farage? Bastard.

 STEPHEN: Gobby bastard.

SANDY & SANDRA, BRIXTON

AMY:

Politicians. Poxy politicians. Stupid idiots who take up the News.

 SANDY: UKIP? He's a dickhead. Don't like him. I don't like anybody who has anything to do with the National Front. I'm sorry, it doesn't work. Not now. Not in 2014. Come on! We're a multicultural country now. We should all get on with each other.

I don't mean to be funny, but all he's doing is these cakes. With raisins, you know? When he has meetings, he always has scones on the table. For the old generation. People with cups of tea. So obviously he's not looking for the younger ones. He's aiming at the older generation. Because the older people are set in their ways, so what he says they will understand.

LEON & JUNE, LIVERPOOL

 JUNE: He's just got one tune. And he keeps on playing it, over and over again. And he never answers any straight question, does he? A lot of his followers are our age, and are still fighting the last war. People who say, 'Our England,' and hate going to London, because 'It's not our capital any more…' And it's not helped by the way some of the media are. You look at the rubbish on the front of the tabloids and think, 'Excuse me. Where's the news?'

LEON: A dickhead. A dangerous dickhead. 'The whole of Bulgaria and Romania are coming.' Yeah. My grandparents were immigrants. Fled the pogroms in Russia. My father fought in the last war with the 8th Army. He was wounded in Sicily. 'They're all right, Indians and West Indians, they're all right to fight for us in the war, but you mustn't have them living here.' Oh, it annoys me. Terrible racist country, we are.

THE SIDDIQUIS, DERBY

 UMAR: I don't know what it is about Nigel Farage, but I just can't take him seriously. I don't know whether it's his policies or his face.

STEPH & DOM, SANDWICH

 STEPH: Enoch Powell by another name.

THE SIDDIQUIS, DERBY

 UMAR: Our future king.

NICK CLEGG

THE SIDDIQUIS, DERBY

 UMAR: Is that Nick Clegg, or an actor playing Nick Clegg?

STEPH & DOM, SANDWICH

 STEPH: He looks like he's got bad breath.

SANDY & SANDRA, BRIXTON

 SANDRA: He's a dickhead trier.

STEPH & DOM, SANDWICH

 STEPH: Imagine that lily-livered little bloody thing running the country.

DOM: How would you use an extra £600 a year?

 STEPH: Two pairs of shoes, darling.

ALEX SALMOND

THE MOFFATTS, COUNTY DURHAM

 SCARLETT: He's not going to get that many votes though, because he's limiting himself, isn't he, calling himself the Scotland party? Because only Scottish people are going to vote for him.

LINDA, PETE & GEORGE, CLACTON-ON-SEA

 PETE: What's the matter with you, you pillock?

PENSIONS

STEPH & DOM, SANDWICH

 DOM: They've sort of screwed the whole thing up and they've got a major problem on their hands. We're all living a lot longer, there are more of us, we're not dying, we're not allowed to die, you're not allowed to kill yourself, and now they've banned smoking, they've done all that so we live a lot longer. You know, at some stage they've got to start lifting a few of the laws to enable us to die off a bit quicker.

THE MICHAELS, BRIGHTON

THE MICHAELS, BRIGHTON

 CAROLYNE: If they stopped putting all their money into Trident, if they stopped putting all their money into these phoney wars, I'd love to know how much money we would have then. I reckon we'd have plenty.

THE WOERDENWEBERS, THE WIRRAL

 RALF: I want Danny Alexander to work a week on the construction. And then, after the week I say to him, 'Listen, you little twat, come here. So, you want to do this fifty years from now? You want to do this when you're sixty-five and seventy? So go in your fucking office and think about it again.'

IMMIGRATION

LEON & JUNE, LIVERPOOL

 LEON: We know Romanians, we know Albanians, we know Polish people who work their socks off. And my grandparents were immigrants. And worked hard.

THE SIDDIQUIS, DERBY

 RAZA: How would you sneak in?

 BAASIT: I'd swim the Channel. I'd get to France and swim the Channel and then creep in.

 RAZA: How did we sneak in last time, Dad?

ANDREW:
I don't really want to be preached to by a multimillionaire private school kid who's going to give us the crumbs off his table to the tune of £600.

Linda, George and Pete
Clacton-on-Sea

Linda,
Pete & George

CLACTON-ON-SEA

———

Linda and Pete, both 64, have been married for
seventeen years. George, 30, moved back in with
his mum and stepdad after separating from his
long-term partner. Ex-publicans Linda and Pete are
both foster carers, having looked after 157 children.
George is known to his friends as 'Squeaky George'
due to his high-pitched voice.

———

HOW DID YOU MEET?

PETE: I used to drink in her first pub, the Woolpack in Witham. I used to go with my late wife. Linda was going through a rough patch with her husband.

LINDA: We got divorced. I've been married three times.

PETE: And unfortunately, my lovely Sue, she died. She had cancer. And that was

it, really. You took another pub on, didn't you, Lin? In Braintree. And I sort of went over there one day. And never come home again.

LINDA: I wouldn't let him go home.

PETE: I sort of disappeared. I just paid the mortgage on my house and that was it.

HOW DID YOU GET ON GOGGLEBOX?

GEORGE: My friend James used to work behind the bar at the social club in St Osyth, near Clacton. And he phoned me up and said, 'I'm working on this programme, and you should do it because it would be perfect for you.' I'd gone through a really bad break-up a couple of years previous. And he said, 'George, you sat at the bar, even though you were depressed, mate, and you were funny. You cheered me up.' I was going to do it with my mate, but halfway through doing the try-out, my mum came in. And she was really funny.

LINDA: George (for some unknown reason) told the Worm Story. Because when he was a little boy, he said, 'How was I born, Mummy?' and I said, 'Well, this worm kept crawling in my kitchen

and I kept throwing it out, and one day I picked it up and it had this cute little George-y face and I thought, "Oh, I'll start feeding this." And that's how you come.' So George told the story: 'So I was seven years old and thought I was a worm,' and I went, 'Wanker!' and all the film crew were laughing. So they wanted me. And then we bullied Pete into it. He's quieter than us.

GEORGE: Pete is a BFG: a big friendly giant. And I don't know why but he goes along with whatever my mum says.

LINDA: We didn't really know what we were getting into, because we'd never seen the show. Even when we were filming, we still didn't know what it was about. We didn't get it.

HOW DID YOU GET ON GOGGLEBOX?

(continued)

Like a lot of people, I thought, 'Ooh, what a weird programme. A bit boring, this.' But I think it's very, very contagious.

After about three times, you get your favourite characters, and you want to see what they have to say. People insist that they don't like it. I say, 'I don't expect you to, but you really have got to watch it three times to get it.'

PETE: We did it for George.

LINDA: He's got such a personality. He's *wasted*. And although he's an electrician, I said to him, 'If you could get paid for entertaining…if you could do something like this, it'd be fantastic rather than getting up in lofts.' You know – when he's got all that talent.

PETE: I want him to get on. So he leaves me a load of money.

LINDA:

…and one day I picked the worm up and it had this cute little George-y face and I thought, 'Oh, I'll start feeding this.'

WHAT DO YOU THINK
OF YOURSELVES ON SCREEN?

GEORGE: When I saw myself, I thought, 'What a cock.'

PETE: I didn't like watching myself at first. I thought, 'Jesus Christ, haven't I put weight on? I can't be in this show.' I thought we were all slim really. I mean, look at that handsome bastard up there, in the wedding photo. Once you get through that stage, it is funny. You're not just cringing at yourself, you're laughing at some of the others. Perversely, you start to enjoy it after a while.

LINDA: I have to go in my own bedroom and sit all quiet and watch it all on my own. To be embarrassed. One time, I was crying, watching myself crying on television. I made myself cry again because I got so emotional.

PETE: When she goes in there, George goes off and watches it on his own, and I'm sitting in here.

LINDA: We all have to watch it on different tellies.

GEORGE: I've got a friend, Gerald, and he talks like Dom, from Steph and Dom, you know? He's very well spoken.

PETE: Gerald is posher than Prince Charles.

LINDA: He's going to teach George to sail.

PETE: That will be a calamity. I can't see George being Captain Kipper.

GEORGE: Anyway, believe it or not, I was planning to sail round, what is it, the Sea of Biscuits? The Bay of Biscay, that's it. With Gerry. And he saw me on the television. And he said, 'Dear boy, you're funny enough as it is. You don't need to accentuate your vocabulary with swear words.' And he made me look at it, and I thought to myself, 'Oh my gawd, I do swear a lot.' But I can't help it. There's a lot of wine in that cup.

BEING RECOGNISED

LINDA: Do you know what we like about this the most? We've met *absolutely lovely* people. People coming up because we've been on telly. We haven't done it to be famous. But, like, solicitors come up, people you wouldn't think. And they've come up to me in Marks & Spencer's and gone, 'You're brilliant on that show.' They can tell you're not acting.

GEORGE: Mum likes it. She deserves it, to be honest. The other day, she came out the back of Williams & Griffin in Colchester, and this lady went, 'Lin! Lin!' And me mum went, 'Yeah,' as if to say, 'Yes, it is me, off the telly...' And the lady went, 'Can you move your car?'

HAVE YOU EVER MET A CELEBRITY?

LINDA: I used to cut Bucks Fizz's hair. I owned a hairdresser's in Rainham called Lindy Lou's. It was very popular. I used to do Mike Nolan's mum and all his family. And on the night before he got famous, he was in. He said, 'I've got someone interested in me, listen to this.' And while I did his highlights (because he was right blond) he put this record on. And I go, 'Ain't she got a good voice?' He went, 'That's me.' I went, 'Oh, you sound like Frankie Valli.'

EVER GOT ANYTHING OUT OF GOGGLEBOX?

PETE: I'm always getting recognised in taxis and they all take your photo, but I've had nobody buy me a beer.

WHAT DOES TV MEAN TO YOU?

GEORGE: I think it's a commodity that needs to be used for a better cause.

LINDA:
I found the kappa tracksuit in a charity shop and the most dreadful trainers.

FANCY DRESS

LINDA: I've done fancy dress as Vicky Pollard. And Su Pollard. Su Pollard was in Rainham Carnival and we won it. I had all the chalet maid's things, I've got photographs of it. And Vicky Pollard I did recently at fancy dress. All shocking pink. I kept going round all night, eating off the buffet going, 'Yeah, I've got me baby parked outside.'

PETE: It was brilliant.

LEON & JUNE, LIVERPOOL

 LEON: *Titanic* made me cry. The ending. And *Pretty Woman*.

 JUNE: I cried at *Quartet*. And unfairness towards people, that makes me upset. The disabled: they're still not getting a fair crack of the whip. And the elderly.

And in *Coronation Street*, the story about Hayley having pancreatic cancer. We were very upset when we saw that. And then we met one of the writers, Jan McVerry, just by chance. She's local. We were having a coffee and she recognised us. And we were so delighted to talk to her. I said how well researched it was, and she came to thank us and for us to pass on thanks to *Gogglebox* for putting it on and for showing everybody's reactions.

I'm sure soaps have to have fires and dramatic things to keep everybody's interest going, but things like cancer do open up the world, because I think in every family somebody is touched, even if not directly.

LINDA, PETE & GEORGE, CLACTON-ON-SEA

 LINDA: Anything to do with animals or children. I cry terrible. I cried at the end of *Educating Yorkshire* with the boy with the stammer. I was ever so upset because George had a stammer when he was a little boy, and that's how I helped him. I used to sing to him, 'Do you want your breakfast, George?'

 PETE: It was like being in an opera.

 LINDA: And he could answer me without stammering, by singing, 'Oh yes please, Mummy…'

 PETE: Now you can't *stop* him talking, can you?

JUNE:

Leon's a great sentimentalist.

THE MICHAELS, BRIGHTON

 ANDREW: *Touched by an Angel.* We were on holiday in Cyprus, watching it, and we were all sobbing our eyes out, weren't we?

 LOUIS: I cried when Miranda nearly died in *Call the Midwife.*

 CAROLYNE: We nearly died that day. We thought she was going to lose the baby.

STEPHEN & CHRIS, BRIGHTON

 CHRIS: The programme on being gay in Russia. That was absolutely awful. It was that whole thing of: you didn't want to watch it, but you had to, because you couldn't believe what was actually going on, and you didn't know whether to cry or be angry.

When I went to bed, I couldn't sleep. And even the next day I felt really affected by it. I was bullied as a kid, and a lot of the people on that programme were being manipulated and bullied by these horrible straight people. And it sort of took me back to when I used to be bullied for being gay.

THE SIDDIQUIS, DERBY

 UMAR: As you get older — I don't know if it's sentimentality or what — but stuff moves you more. The bit right at the end of the last *Lord of the Rings* film. *The Return of the King.*

 BAASIT: They have that big-ass war and Frodo's gone through all that stuff and Aragorn becomes the king and they're just humbly standing there and they bow in front of him. And he says, 'You bow for no man.' And the whole kingdom bows for those guys. It's done really well.

 UMAR: I think you appreciate what the film is trying to tell you.

 BAASIT: Don't trust short people. Because they'll kick your ass.

STEPH & DOM, SANDWICH

 STEPH: After you become a parent, your own mortality suddenly becomes very real. We tend to cry at anything to do with loss of child, loss of parent – loss of any kind. Any cancers, illness – can't cope with it. And if we see it's in the description, we won't watch it on that very basis: that we know it'll absolutely kill us. Tug at our heart strings.

JOSH:

Surprise Surprise. With Holly Willoughby. It's emotional.

 DOM: There was a time almost every film that we chose had a background story about a woman losing her mother or someone dying of cancer.

 STEPH: And I'd only just lost my mother. And it was a bit like when you buy a car and you suddenly see loads of them on the road. I remember taking a DVD to Mother in hospital so we could sit and watch it together in the afternoon, and it was about a woman losing her mother to cancer, but it didn't say that in the beginning, so we're both sitting there watching it, and I suddenly went, 'Waaahhh,' and my mother's going, 'This is really horrible!' We didn't turn it off though. And luckily, she had a great sense of humour, so she was like, 'Oh well, we're halfway through it, let's see what happens in the end.' 'We fucking know what's going to happen in the end, Mum! She's going to die!' It's a bit like watching *Jesus Christ Superstar*. 'What happens in the end?'

I do remember having a conversation with somebody (who shall remain unnamed) about the film *The Passion of the Christ*. I was explaining about the film and she said, 'My God, it sounds amazing. What happened in the end?' Mind you, Dom cries at *Lassie*.

 DOM: Yeah…

 STEPH: He's a total poof now. I thought you were going last night.

 DOM: Yeah…there was one tiny little tear. At the end of the wedding scene, or something. Whatever it was.

STEPH: But everybody was *so happy.*

 DOM: It got emotional. And, bloody hell, I'm sitting there, top lip starts going and, you know…

 STEPH: Oh, God. It was so funny.

 DOM: … and I was very tired.

 NIKKI: We're a little bit soft in this house.

 AMY: We're always crying at the TV. Always. There was one programme that we watched and it was just the most depressing thing I've ever sat through. It was basically a bunch of pensioners, with dementia or something wrong with them, and they were just dying. And it was just the most horrendous thing to watch. And I cried the whole way through it. Tears down my face. Non-stop.

 NIKKI: I'll make another cup of tea.

THE MOFFATTS, COUNTY DURHAM

 SCARLETT: And, you know, *Comic Relief* and that, where they have those African kids and they have flies all in their eyes and that? We don't cry at chick flicks, though, do we? Like *Titanic* and all that. Just charity appeals. I once started crying at the train station, ended up giving £11 a month. That was for cats. I don't even like cats.

CAROLYNE:

Dallas, when JR got shot. Bloody hell. Cry? Devastated.

Or those donkey adverts. It's got a limp, it's so sad, and it's been working for eighteen hours a day and you're just, like, 'That poor donkey.' It just wants to chill out and it can't. Because they're just dragging it around. It wants to chill out, with carrots, like on the beach or whatever. It's got hooves and sad eyes. I don't like seeing people with sad eyes.

REV. KATE & GRAHAM, NOTTINGHAMSHIRE

KATE: They showed us something on *Gogglebox* which was a Sports Relief thing where there was an older gentleman whose wife had died, and Sports Relief were funding a phone line for him to be able to talk to other people. And apparently when they showed it to all the *Gogglebox*ers, they were all sobbing, because this old guy was really lonely and he was crying.

That didn't affect me really. Because what affects me more is the actual guy who I go and visit, whose wife died last year, who I go and have a cup of tea with, and who comes to church. Because he's real. And that upsets me.

I don't cry for the telly. Part of my own therapy is watching telly. Because I do such a crazy job. One minute I can be stood in assembly dressed as an Oompa Loompa on World Book Day, and half an hour later – *literally half an hour later* – I can be burying a baby. And I don't cry the days when I carry a dead baby into church. Of course I don't. But when I come home from a really difficult funeral, I open a bottle of wine, hug the kids extra tight, and watch really crap TV.

And that's the power of television. It has the power to move you to tears, to stimulate conversation, to help you to relax. It's the most powerful thing in anyone's sitting room.

And that's why, when people said to me, 'Oh, *Gogglebox*, what a stupid idea for a show, it's about watching people watching telly…' Well, you've missed the point of the show. Because it's actually about *watching people*.

That's what it's about.

People.

A MEETING

 CAROLYNE: One day I was in a supermarket car park in Brighton, and I had a trolley. And the car park had been shut, so in order to get my £1 coin back I had to wheel the trolley all the way outside the supermarket, down a side street and then up a whole flight of stairs.

 CHRIS: I was in Morrisons car park and I was walking down this big row of concrete steps. And there was this woman pulling this trolley up the bloody steps.

 CAROLYNE: So I was dragging this trolley up some stairs, really with a lot of difficulty...

 CHRIS: So I turned round and said, 'Would you like a hand with that, love?'

 CAROLYNE: ...and I heard this voice say, 'Can I help you with that, love?' And I thought, 'It's Chris!'

 CHRIS: And she sort of looked at me and she went 'Oh, Chris!'

 CAROLYNE: And he looked at me and I looked at him.

 CHRIS: And I thought, 'Oh God! Is it some crank? Have I done her hair?' And then I noticed the pink lipstick and the penny dropped: it was Carolyne from the Michaels.

 CAROLYNE: And we both said, 'It's YOU!' And we had this huge hug.

 CHRIS: So I had a good old chat with her. She was lovely. Absolutely lovely.

 CAROLYNE: Honestly, it was like meeting an old friend.

ACKNOWLEDGEMENTS

A book like this doesn't happen on its own. It needs lots of help. And this book had a lot of help from a lot of lovely people. And when lovely people are helpful, it's polite to say thank you.

So, thank you, first, to Rev. Kate and Graham; Sid, Umar and Baasit; Mark, Betty and Scarlett; Leon and June; Ralf, Viv, Eve and Jay; Bill and Josef; Linda, Pete and George; Stephen and Chris; Sandy and Sandra; Andrew, Carolyne, Louis and Alex; Jonathan, Nikki, Josh and Amy; and Steph and Dom. Without their help, this book would have been embarrassingly short.

Second helpings of thank you to Tania Alexander, Melissa Bartlett and Gemma Scholes at Studio Lambert; Katy Follain and Natasha Hodgson at Canongate; Anne Miles at transcripts4u; intrepid researcher and spreadsheet maven Victoria Thomas; TV historian and all-round good egg Joe Moran; and the formidable Cat Ledger, for whom the word 'agent' was surely invented.

Last but not least, special thanks go to the wonderful David Glover and those lovely people at Channel 4 for their continual love and support.